D0804315

A
VERY
PRESENT
HELP

A
VERY PRESENT
HELP

Psalm Studies for Older Adults

Miriam Dunson

Geneva Press
Louisville, Kentucky

© 1999 Miriam Dunson

All rights reserved. No part of this book may be reproduced or transmitted in any form or by any means, electronic or mechanical, including photocopying, recording, or by any information storage or retrieval system, without permission in writing from the publisher. For information, address Geneva Press, 100 Witherspoon Street, Louisville, Kentucky 40202-1396.

Unless otherwise indicated, scripture quotations are from the New Revised Standard Version of the Bible, copyright © 1989 by the Division of Christian Education of the National Council of the Churches of Christ in the U. S. A., and are used by permission.

Scripture quotations from the Revised Standerd Version of the Bible are copyrighted 1946, 1952, © 1971, 1973 by the Division of Christian Education of the National Council of the Churches of Christ in the U.S.A. and are used by permission.

Scripture quotations marked NIV are from the Holy Bible, New International Version. Copyright © 1973, 1978, 1984 International Bible Society. Used by permission of Zondervan Bible Publishers

Book design by Sharon Adams
Cover design by Pam Poll

First edition
Published by Geneva Press
Louisville, Kentucky

This book is printed on acid-free paper that meets the American National Standards Institute Z39.48 standard. ♾

PRINTED IN THE UNITED STATES OF AMERICA

99 00 01 02 03 04 05 06 07 08—10 9 8 7 6 5 4 3 2 1

Library of Congress Cataloging-in-Publication Data

Dunson, Miriam.
 A very present help : Psalm studies for older adults / by Miriam
 Dunson.
  p.   cm.
 Includes bibliographical references.
 ISBN 0-664-50034-X (alk. paper)
 1. Bible. O.T. Psalms—Study and teaching. 2. Christian aged—
 Religious life. I. Title.
 BS1430.5.D86 1999
 232'.2'0071—dc21   99-23298

Dedicated to My Parents
Whose faith drew me to the Psalms
Whose life and aging I found echoed in the Psalms

My father, Henry H. Dunson,
who died in 1985, and who lives on most keenly
in the many ways he found to build up
the church and the community, and in the values
he passed on to his family

and

My mother, Joyce G. Dunson,
who at the age of ninety-two continues to bring joy
to my life, and a beautiful model for
gracious aging

A CELEBRATION

This book is written in part as my contribution to the celebration of the United Nations International Year of Older Persons in 1999 under the theme, "Toward a Society for All Ages." By taking this action the United Nations invites study, education, and action on matters related to the present and future status of older persons in societies around the world. The United Nations Principles for Older Persons, as identified in the UN resolution, include Independence, Participation, Care, Self-fulfillment, and Dignity.

In response to the resolution of the United Nations, the 210th General Assembly of the Presbyterian Church (U.S.A.) (1998) approved a resolution encouraging support, participation, and celebration throughout the church.

This book is written as a contribution to add a spiritual dimension to the UN action, and to provide materials for older persons that may bring a new perspective to life in the later years and empowerment to their lives as they seek to serve God for the rest of their years.

CONTENTS

FOREWORD

How many times I have wished for a Bible study guide as I work with older persons in various settings. Whether leading a Bible study group in a health care center or teaching classes for older persons in a local congregation, I have found a glaring lack of guides that relate scripture to the unique needs of older persons. Miriam Dunson's *A Very Present Help: Psalm Studies for Older Adults* addresses this deficiency. Here at last are studies where God's story in scripture and the stories of older persons find real connection.

Miriam's experience in leading Bible studies as a chaplain at Wesley Woods Homes in Atlanta, Georgia, and her dedicated experience with older adult ministry has uniquely qualified her to write this book. Miriam knows older people; she has "sat where they sit," not as a disinterested observer, but as a friend and spiritual director.

But thousands of books have been written about the Psalms. Why another? Simply because this is a book that connects the Psalms with the needs and life situations of older persons. As expressed by the author, the purpose of this book is, "to provide materials for older persons that may bring a new perspective to life in the later years and empowerment to their lives as they seek to serve God for the rest of their years."

As we struggle with the new problems of graying into the twenty-first century, we need to be enabled to live fully through the life of the spirit.

The writer of the First Psalm knew well where the blessedness of life was found. "But his [her] delight is in the law of the LORD, and on his law he [she] meditates day and night" (Psalm 1:2, NIV). This is a book that helps older persons do just that. The format is clear and easy to follow. A compelling introduction, with many chapters sprinkled with some of Miriam's own experiences, captures your interest. The background of the psalm, its meaning, and how it relates to older persons opens avenues for rich study and reflection. Helpful discussion questions and notes for the group leader offer further help.

Miriam discusses the "roller coaster world" of older persons, and her choice of ten psalms mirrors this experience for older persons. The Psalms tell the story of those who wound their way through sorrow to joy, through darkness to light, through death to resurrection. As the book suggests, there are times of calm as-surance and feelings of integrity, but at other times, there is dis-location, marginalization, a search for new identities and redirection, and a deep concern for care. All of these experiences are mirrored in the Psalms. As one resident in Miriam's group ex-pressed it, "If the psalmist said it, perhaps it is all right for me to say it if that's the way I feel!"

One senses a constant note of pastoral care for God's oldest friends in this book. The author does not gloss over the ambi-guities of aging. Growing older may well mean experiencing new freedom and new evidences of God's grace, but the last decades of life may also puzzle us, if not torment us with the losses and pain that threaten us. Miriam shows how God is ever present, bringing comfort, strength, and wisdom to get through the difficult times.

Although the primary purpose of this book is for group study, older persons who do not have access to groups would also ben-efit from private reading and study of the Psalms. However it may be used, Miriam's book opens new doors for spiritual en-richment for older persons. Some older people are soaked in the scriptures. Others are not. But, regardless of their biblical knowl-edge, all will be amazed at how these ancient psalms sound like pages ripped from their own experience.

In her book, Miriam Dunson offers a rich study of ten psalms. But the book points beyond itself to an opportunity for spiritual renewal, in which God offers us 150 psalms for our growth and enrichment. This book can become the road to a renewed read-ing and study of this "prayerbook of the Bible," and no greater need exists for older people as life winds down than a deepened spiritual life.

These deep expressions of love and longing come out of the experience of people who were seeking the God who was seek-ing them. This is what this book helps older people discover—that regardless of whatever life has dealt them, they are not alone. God is a very present help in time of trouble.

Richard L. Morgan
Presbyterian minister, author, and Parish Associate
for Older Adults, First Presbyterian Church,
Morganton, North Carolina

PREFACE

Older adults (age 65 and over) now comprise the fastest growing segment of the population of the United States. In addition to the physical limitations that sometimes accompany the aging process, older adults must also face the difficulties of living in a society that has no clear place for them. They must face the negative attitudes of a youth-oriented, production-driven culture. They live in a society in which the question no longer is "What can I give?" but "What can I get?"

This is a foreign concept to those who grew up during the Great Depression, from the 1920s to the start of World War II. In addition, many older adults, who have been surrounded by family and friends in all other transition and crisis times of life, find that they must face perhaps the most difficult phase of their lives alone. Left alone by the death of a spouse, with adult children living their own lives elsewhere, many older adults find that feelings of loneliness and isolation are a part of everyday life.

During an intern year as chaplain in a retirement community, I became aware of such feelings on the part of some of the residents. I also observed that there was little communication among the residents concerning their life joys and struggles. I decided to experiment with using the Psalms as the basis of a Bible study series with the residents, with the hope that a sharing, supportive community would develop within the study group that could provide a measure of pastoral caring for all in the group. The response was such that I began to believe I was onto something significant.

The value in studying the Psalms seemed to be that the words of the psalmist could many times supply the participants with the exact words to fit their situation when they could not find the words for themselves. Further, when they were reluctant to express negative feelings, the participants reminded themselves, "If the psalmist said it, perhaps it is all right for me to say it if that's the way I feel."

The response of the participants to a study of the Psalms was enthusiastic and immediate. Half an hour was soon determined to be too short for the study of a psalm, and so a second meeting of one hour in the afternoon of the same day was decided upon to reflect upon the study and to deal with the issues raised. This response was such that it could be assumed that at least in some measure, some needs of the residents were being met by this study of the Psalms. The group grew in number and in enthusiasm, and a warm trusting community developed among the members. Some close relationships developed, some loneliness dissipated, and the group members began to experience the group as a safe place in which to share their struggles and their joys. I became convinced that there is a close and abiding link between the issues raised by the ancient hymn writers and the issues that older adults deal with on a daily basis. It was this experience that led me to write my doctoral dissertation on the subject, "Pastoral Care with Older Adults through the Psalms." This experience has also led me to write this series of Bible studies based on the Psalms for use by older persons, either for individual or group study. The book is a topical study, each chapter focused on a chosen topic and based on a psalm. It is offered with the hope that all who read the book can experience Paul's description in 2 Corinthians 4:7–10: "But we have this treasure in jars of clay to show that this all-surpassing power is from God and not from us. We are hard pressed on every side, but not crushed; perplexed, but not in despair; persecuted, but not abandoned; struck down, but not destroyed. We always carry around in our body the death of Jesus, so that the life of Jesus may also be revealed in our body" (NIV).

ACKNOWLEDGMENTS

I am grateful to Ed Craxton, Associate Director of the Christian Education Program Area in the Congregational Ministries Division, who granted permission for me to write this book as an older adult ministry resource.

I am especially grateful to Marvin Simmers, Coordinator of the Pastor, Educator, and Lay Leader Support Program Team, who provided the impetus, the stimulation, and the encouragement that caused this writing to take place. His many editorial skills, his innate ability to run interference for me so that I could write the book and his own strong, contagious, and caring spiritual leadership has made the idea of this book become a reality.

As I write this book, I continue to be grateful for the residents at Wesley Woods Homes in Atlanta who became my good friends during a seminary intern year when we explored the Psalms in such a thorough and exciting manner.

I am so grateful to my family; my mother, Joyce Dunson, is ninety-two years of age as I write this, and has aged graciously, kindly, and with real class, although experiencing many of the diminishments that sometimes come with the aging process. She and my sister, Barbara Bender, have brought much encouragement and enthusiasm to me as I have taken on this project.

Richard Morgan has been a guiding light in my writing this book. His suggestions for improvement all along the way, and especially his encouraging words, have been greatly appreciated.

The staff of Geneva Press have been most helpful, gracious, and patient with me in working through this, my first effort at book publication. My gratitude to them is great.

Royalties from the sale of this book will be donated to the Presbyterian Church (U.S.A.) Foundation for the Permanent Fund (Endowment) for Older Adult Ministry. Readers who would like to help ensure the long-term continuation of Older Adult Ministry in the Presbyterian Church (U.S.A.) can direct their gifts to the Presbyterian Foundation, Gift Administration, 200 E. 12th St., Jeffersonville, Indiana 47130. Gifts should be specifically designated for Older Adult Ministry, Account No. 3290052-58345.

PREPARATION FOR STUDYING THE PSALMS

Throughout this study, the suggestion is made to read the psalms in the many different translations and paraphrases that are available for the purpose of understanding as clearly as possible the meaning of the verses at the time they were written, as well as discerning what meaning there might be for our lives today.

In preparation for this series of studies, I would suggest that you gather the following to keep on hand for reference:

New Revised Standard Version Bible (NRSV)
Revised Standard Version Bible (RSV)
The Holy Bible: New International Version (NIV)
The New Jerusalem Bible (NJB)
The Jerusalem Bible (JB)
Good News Bible: Today's English Version (TEV)
Psalms Now, A Paraphrase by Leslie Brandt
The Message: Psalms by Eugene H. Peterson

Chapter 1

WHY THE PSALMS?

The reason why the Church loves the Psalms, then, is not merely that they have been sent to her by God from His far-distant heaven, but because God has given Himself to her in them, as though in a sacrament. The Church loves to sing over and over again the songs of the old psalmists because in them she is singing of her knowledge of God, of her union with Him.

—Thomas Merton

Why were the Psalms chosen as the basis of these Bible studies for older persons? Is there some special link between the issues addressed by the ancient hymn writers and those that are a part of the everyday lives of older persons? I believe the answer to this question is a resounding and enthusiastic "Yes." The reason is that although this ancient hymnbook speaks to all ages in a powerful manner, it speaks to older persons in a very personal way. Older readers often exclaim while studying the Psalms, "That's exactly how I feel!" It might be helpful to explore this discovery further.

People of faith down through the ages have recognized the unique way in which the Psalms speak to the innermost feelings of the readers. Martin Luther said, "The Psalter is the favorite book of all the saints."[1] In explaining why he believed this to be true, he said, "Each person, whatever his circumstance may be, finds in the Psalms words which are appropriate to the circumstances in which he finds himself, and meet his needs as adequately as if they were composed exclusively for his sake."[2] In his commentary on the Psalms, John Calvin went even further in his praises of the Psalms by describing them as "an anatomy of all parts of the soul. . . . [T]here is not an emotion of which anyone can be conscious that is not here represented as in a mirror."[3] St. Augustine called the Psalms, "the looking glass of the soul."[4] William Holladay writes, "For two millennia, this collection of 150 individual psalms has helped to shape the public and private worship of Jews and Christians; I am not aware of any other body of religious poetry that has been so influential for so long a period of time, and for such a variety of religious communities."[5]

These thoughts from the past and the present indicate that it is not a new idea that the Psalter is unique in providing expression for the ups and downs of everyday life for all ages. But perhaps they give expression especially to the thoughts and feelings experienced by persons in the later years of life.

The Psalter, as we now read it, is often known as the Hymnbook of the Second Temple. This is not to suggest that the book of Psalms is a product of the postexilic period; rather the postexilic period saw the collecting and collating of the cultic communal liturgies of many, many years. Some perhaps began as early as David, or even earlier.

Some may say that the Psalms are not realistic. Psalm 23, for example, is thought by some to be naive when it says, "The LORD is my shepherd, I shall not want," especially in view of all the cruelty, violence, hunger, and suffering in the world, and that to study the psalm only supports an unrealistic view of the world. Others may say that the Psalms give a picture of God that is vengeful, as in Psalm 137: "Happy shall be he who takes your little ones and dashes them against the rock" (v. 9).

It is accurate to say that some of the Old Testament ideas reflected in the Psalms are repulsive to the twentieth-century mind. It is also true that the thoughts and feelings expressed by the psalmists in their particular circumstances were real, and may not be very different from the anguish expressed by twentieth-century believers following a particularly devastating experience, or from the anger created when twentieth-century believers are faced with some of the senseless atrocities that happen in the modern world. Therefore, this book is based on the belief that the Psalms are indeed in touch with the realities of life.

TYPES OF PSALMS

Keeping in mind the emotional, social, and spiritual dimensions of later life, a review of the various types of psalms and identification of the themes that run throughout the Psalms may be helpful before beginning the specific study of the Psalms.

The beginning of modern research on the Psalms was led by Hermann Gunkel in 1926 when he attempted to classify psalms according to literary types.[6] The form-critical method Gunkel used has been criticized, although the criticism tends to be more about detail than structure. In his guide to the Psalms, John Day says, "In broad terms, the main outlines of Gunkel's classificatory system may still be followed, though there is always scope for disagreement about details."[7] Despite the criticism, Gunkel's classification of the Psalms is helpful in identifying the themes and the wide variety of emotions expressed in the Psalms; and so, his classifications are reflected here.

"Psalms of praise" usually consist of a call to praise, followed by a statement of the reason for praise and a renewed summons to praise God for God's goodness and faithfulness. Some of the more familiar psalms of praise are Psalm 8 and Psalm 103, a study of which is included in this book. Others in this category are Psalm 100 and Psalm 150. Many of our most beloved hymns are based on psalms of praise, such as "All People That on Earth Do Dwell," based on Psalm 100, and "Bless the Lord, O My Soul," based on Psalm 103.

The "hymns of Zion" were directed toward the temple on Mount Zion, not directly to God, although the temple was seen as the earthly dwelling place of the Lord and so these hymns were in reality praises for the presence of God. Included in these hymns are Psalms 46, 48, 76, and 87. In modern hymnbooks, "God Is Our Refuge and Our Strength" is one of the familiar hymns that is based on Psalm 46.

> *There is a river whose streams make glad the city of God, the holy habitation of the Most High. (46:4)*

The "enthronement psalms," including Psalms 29, 47, 93, and others, have to do with God's sovereignty. God's triumph over chaos and calamity is found throughout these psalms.

Kings rise and fall, but God continues as the sovereign ruler over God's creation.

> *The LORD sits enthroned over the flood; the LORD sits enthroned as king forever. May the LORD give strength to his people! May the LORD bless his people with peace! (29:10–11).*

The "psalms of lament" form the largest group, approximately 40 of the 150 hymns. These appeal to God for divine help out of situations that are overwhelming, such as expressed in Psalm 130:1: "Out of the depths I cry to you, O LORD." These psalms are about the crises of life, about times when conditions are encountered by individuals that threaten their well-being or even their existence, and challenge their faith. Here the psalmist gives free vent to frustrations, anger, hurt, and anguish. Usually, toward the end of the psalms of lament, the author moves on to express confidence in God and assurance that God has given him a favorable hearing.

One of the most striking features of these psalms of lament could be called the "pendulum swing." The mood changes from utter despair to soaring confidence, sometimes several times within one hymn. The most familiar psalms in this category are Psalms 22, 42, 43, 51, 102, and 103. So strong are the evidences of trust in these psalms that one might be tempted to call them "hymns of trust" rather than "psalms of lament."

The psalms in which the lament is individual are filled with anguish, anger, and pleading for God to intervene. As Walter Brueggemann describes, "Something is amiss in the relationship and it must be righted."[8] These psalms include Psalms 13, 35, 86, and others.

Included in the psalms of lament are several in which the whole community seeks the safety of the temple and the protection of the sovereign God. Examples of these community laments are Psalms 12, 44, 58, 60, and 137. Psalm 137, included in these Bible studies, is a hymn of the exiles in Babylon, expressing utter despair and grief over their losses: "By the waters of Babylon, there we sat down and wept, when we remembered Zion" (v. 1, RSV). In strange surroundings, away from the familiar, they remembered and they wept.

It is here among psalms of lament that many of the cries are of aloneness, that God is not present, as in "Will you forget me forever?" (13:1). The experience described is total aloneness: "I'm alone—help me, and I'm angry because I am alone—how long is this going to continue?" I believe that the theme of aloneness, so dominant in the Psalms as well as in the lives of many older persons, is one of the major links between the Psalms and the issues many older adults face.

"Psalms of confidence" may be the most familiar of the psalms. They include Psalms 23, 27, 121, and 131. Even in the midst of deepest anguish confidence in God is reflected. To study these psalms is to study those attributes of the nature of God in which human beings can find their hope in the direst of circumstances.

> *I lift up my eyes to the hills—from where will my help come?*
> *My help comes from the LORD, who made heaven and earth.*
> *(121:1)*

"Psalms of thanksgiving" include Psalms 30, 32, 34, 41, 66, and others. These are related to the psalms of lament in that they look back on the times of distress and chaos, but from the perspective of deliverance, in calmness and in security. The alienation and isolation is remembered, along with the bitterness, but the bitterness has been removed by the restoration of communion with God.

> *Make a joyful noise to God, all the earth; sing the glory of his*
> *name; give to him glorious praise. (66:1)*

The "royal psalms" include Psalms 2, 20, 45, 72, and 110 as the most familiar. There was no separation of church and state in ancient Israel, and the king was a religious as well as a political figure. These psalms were to glorify the kings, but the psalmists sensed in their kings the anticipation of a real king whom God would surely provide for God's people, and this hope is reflected in the royal psalms.

> *Your throne, O God, endures forever and ever. Your royal*
> *scepter is a scepter of equity. (45:6)*

The "wisdom psalms" are not as easily identified as some others. However, they do include some of the most familiar ones, such as Psalms 1, 37, and 133. Characteristics include a contrasting of the righteous and the wicked, the light with the darkness, and the good with the evil.

> *Trust in the LORD and do good; so you will live in the land, and enjoy security. (37:3)*

While some scholars would argue that all or most of the psalms were used as liturgical texts for temple worship, there are specific psalms that seem to have been sung in services of worship and accompanied by music. Some might be called "liturgical psalms," such as Psalms 24 and 121, probably sung in services of worship in the temple, and "pilgrim psalms," such as Psalms 84 and 122, probably sung by pilgrims when they gathered for the annual festivals.

> *Lift up your heads, O gates! and be lifted up, O ancient doors! that the King of glory may come in. (24:7)*

> *I was glad when they said to me, "Let us go to the house of the LORD!" Our feet are standing within your gates, O Jerusalem. (122:1–2)*

There are some psalms that do not easily fit into a category, such as Psalms 4, 27, 36, and others. Some psalms fit into more than one category. And, of course, some psalms are found to be more poignant for older adults than others. However, this look at the different categories of psalms has begun to demonstrate why the Psalms seem particularly full of meaning, not only for younger persons and middle-aged persons, but especially for older adults.

THEMES IN THE PSALMS

The theme of *remembering* is found throughout the psalms.

> *By the rivers of Babylon—there we sat down and there we wept when we remembered Zion. (137:1)*

> *These things I remember, as I pour out my soul: how I went with the throng, and led them in procession to the house of God. (42:4)*

Seeking and finding *assurance and comfort* is a theme in many of the most familiar psalms, such as Psalm 27: "The LORD is my light and my salvation; whom shall I fear?" (v. 1) or Psalm 46: "God is our refuge and strength, a very present help in trouble" (v. 1).

A theme in the psalms that is often overlooked, because it is deemed to be unpleasant, is *anger.* The expression of the anger of God and the anger of the psalmist is a significant part of the psalms, especially the psalms of lament. Anger against God is a dominant theme, most frequently expressed in the form of the question "Why?" Another expression of anger against God is in the question "How long?" Besides anger against God, there is anger against "the enemy." Although anger does have destructive possibilities, anger also signifies that something important is going on. Anger can help to provoke change or a turning point in relationships with other human beings or with God. It can open up the possibility of growth, reconciliation, and change in the direction of the wholeness sought. For the older adult, much of the anger is against "enemies" such as death that takes away friends and family, and illness that limits activity and isolates one from others.

The theme of *forgiveness and God's mercy* is found in many of the psalms. In Psalm 51 the psalmist pleads, "Have mercy on me, O God. . . . [B]lot out my transgressions. Wash me thoroughly from my iniquity, and cleanse me from my sin. . . . Create in me a clean heart, O God, and put a new and right spirit within me" (vv. 1–2, 10).

Forgiveness in the Psalms has to do with removing the barriers between God and human beings. We were made to live in communion with God and in community with other human beings. Sin and guilt can harm both relationships. God's forgiveness restores communion with God and opens the way for harmonious relationships with other human beings.

Forgiveness is significant for older adults because of the prevalence of guilt feelings concerning goals not reached in life, difficulties in present relationships, or any number of other reasons. Sometimes older persons do not know why they feel guilty, only that they do.

Finally, the theme of *fear* is found throughout the Psalms. Fear is sometimes identified as fear of "the enemy" as in Psalm 64:1b: "Preserve my life from dread of the enemy" (RSV). Sometimes the fear of death is expressed, as in Psalm 23:4: "Even though I walk through the valley of the shadow of death" (RSV). In Psalm 46:2, "We will not fear, though the earth should change," refers to the fear of change.

There are, of course, other themes to be found in the Psalms. The ones identified thus far as the most significant have to do with feelings of being alienated, abandoned, neglected, or rejected. There are the themes of looking back and remembering in order to face the present and the future, of seeking assurance and comfort in the midst of chaos. The theme of anger is followed by repentance, forgiveness, and cleansing.

Gratitude to God and praise for God's deliverance in the past and the hope of God's deliverance in the future run throughout the book of Psalms. The psalmists have very much the same feelings as human beings in the twentieth century. There seems to be a particular correlation between these feelings identified in the psalms and those feelings that many older adults deal with daily. Some older adults feel, as did the psalmists, separated from all that used to be, as though in a foreign land. Some cling to memories of how things used to be. Many are in the midst of transition and change, and find that they are facing it alone.

Of course, all human beings, regardless of age, can and do experience these same feelings. However, could it be that such feelings are intensified during the transitions related to the aging process in older adults? Could it be that in many situations the older adult must face these transitions completely alone? Could it be that this is the link now identified between these ancient hymns and older adults?

The answer of the psalmists over and over again is to remind us of God's sovereign rule. God is in control, God is our constant companion, and we human beings are not and will never be left completely alone. As a hymn writer of more recent times has written:

> The soul that on Jesus hath leaned for repose,
> I will not, I will not desert to its foes;
> That soul, though all hell should endeavor to shake,
> I'll never, no, never, no, never forsake.
>
> ("How Firm a Foundation")

HELPS FOR GROUP STUDY

1. Ask group members to name five psalms that have meant the most to them during their lifetime, then to explain why.
2. Ask each member to choose one of the five and read it aloud to the group, telling why it is important to him or her.
3. Ask the group: Why do you think the Psalms have come to mean so much to both the religious and the secular worlds?
4. Some themes were identified in Chapter 1. Ask: What are some other themes found in the Psalms that have meaning for you?
5. Choose five psalms at random and ask the group to identify in which category of psalms each one falls, such as psalms of lament, praise, Zion, and so forth.

Notes

1. Martin Luther, *Preface to the German Psalter* (1528) quoted in Artur Weiser, *The Psalms* (Philadelphia: Westminster Press, 1962), 20.
2. Ibid.
3. John Calvin, *Commentary on the Psalms,* quoted in Herbert Lockyer, *God's Book of Poetry* (Nashville: Thomas Nelson Publishers, 1983), 9.
4. Ibid.
5. William L. Holladay, *The Psalms through Three Thousand Years* (Minneapolis: Fortress Press, 1993), 1.
6. Hermann Gunkel, *Einleitung in Die Psalmen,* completed and published by J. Begrich (Göttingen, 1933), described in Claus Westermann, *Praise and Lament in the Psalms* (Atlanta: John Knox Press, 1965), 16.
7. John Day, *Psalms* (Sheffield: JSOT Press, 1992), 14.
8. Walter Brueggemann, *The Message of the Psalms: A Theological Commentary*, Old Testament Studies (Minneapolis: Augsburg Publishing House, 1984), 58.

Chapter 2

Psalms 137 and 46
THE WORLD HAS CHANGED
AND SO HAVE I

*As a people, the Hebrews—both ancient and
modern—never forgot this. Even when captured by
the conquering armies of Nebuchadnezzar, who
exiled them to Babylon, even in the ghettoes and
in the camps, they praised and gave thanks to their
God, Yahweh. They created the biblical book
called the Psalms.*

—Maria Harris

INTRODUCTION

The appropriate starting place for this study seems to be the
crisis that eventually produced Judaism as we know it. Most
scholars trace the beginning of Judaism to the crisis precipitated
by the exile in Babylonia, which began with the capture of Jerusalem in 587 B.C.E. This was the second deportation to Babylon,
when King Nebuchadnezzar finally razed Jerusalem to the
ground after a brief respite and intrigue-filled ten years. There
can be no question concerning the date of the writing of Psalm
137, since it is about this specific historical event. The date can
be set with some accuracy. It had to have been written after the
fall of Jerusalem in 587 B.C.E. and before the restoration of the
temple in 515 B.C.E.

To set the stage for these Bible studies I have chosen to look
at Psalms 137 and 46 together. Psalm 137 expresses the anguish
of the Israelites sitting in exile in Babylon yearning for Jerusalem and the temple, which was seen as the dwelling place of
God. This psalm looks back on the fall of Jerusalem, and expresses in vivid images the time of exile in Babylon, and how it

feels to be in a captive situation. Psalm 46, as the first of the songs of Zion, emphasizes the significance of Jerusalem in the lives of God's people. The hymn is not so much about the inviolability of Jerusalem. "Its true subject," according to James Mays, "is the God who will help the people in whose midst God has chosen to be and who for a time chose Jerusalem and its temple as the locale of his 'dwelling place.'"[1] Psalm 46 was the inspiration for Martin Luther's hymn "A Mighty Fortress Is Our God," which sets forth the fact that Zion is stable and secure, in spite of the chaos that is evident in the lives of the people. According to verses 2–3, even though all is in turmoil there is no need to fear.

The people speaking in these psalms were in exile; they had been forced to leave their homeland and were now grieving over their losses while sitting on the banks of the Tigris and Euphrates rivers. They had either seen or heard of the devastation of the temple, and their grief was deep and painful.

The exile had extraordinary faith repercussions. Prior to this event the people of Israel were firmly convinced that their land was God-given, a land of promise and covenant. Their king was God's representative, a sign of divine blessing. The temple, central to Jerusalem, was God's dwelling place. The belief that Jerusalem was inviolable (i.e., not to be violated or dishonored) is clear in Psalm 46:4–5: "There is a river whose streams make glad the city of God, the holy habitation of the Most High. God is in the midst of the city; it shall not be moved; God will help it when the morning dawns."

The temple was Israel's absolute security. Whatever happened, the temple—the dwelling place of the Holy One of Israel—would stand. Therefore, the city of which the temple was the center would never fall.

The firmness of this belief cannot be underestimated. Jerusalem was indeed a natural stronghold. Kings such as Hezekiah had ensured a constant water supply. In order to provide water for the temple, as well as for the city, the Siloam Tunnel was cut through 1,777 feet of hard limestone underneath the mountain on which Jerusalem sat. The tunnel brought water from a spring outside Jerusalem to a pool inside the city wall, a major accomplishment. Under Josiah in 621 B.C.E. the temple was established as the focus for the three main festivals of the year. The temple was the place of sacrificial worship as well as the focus for Passover, covenant renewal, and the festival of firstfruits.

Thus, when Jerusalem fell and its leaders and artisans were deported, their faith and existence were called into question. From the time of Abraham they had been promised a land. The land was the gift of God who had graciously called out a chosen captive people to be God's own. The shepherd king, God's representative, was responsible for political and religious guidance. The temple, where the king also exercised religious duties, was the heartbeat of the faith life of this called-out people.

The presence of the gods of other nations did not trouble Israel. They only had to remind themselves of their sacred history to know again the call of the psalmist:

> "Be still, and know that I am God!
> I am exalted among the nations,
> I am exalted in the earth."
> The LORD of hosts is with us;
> the God of Jacob is our refuge.
> (46:10–11)

Israel truly believed that Jerusalem, its temple, and its God-given dynasty of David would never end.

We might smile at this seemingly simplistic view, but part of us recognizes it. For most of our lives we see ourselves as inviolable. A personal tragedy, death, illness, or war may touch some of us in our younger years, but it is only in our later years that we begin to recognize that this invincible city—our Zion, ourselves—is vulnerable. This is true of people of faith as well as for people of no faith. It is a universal condition. But people of faith will take special comfort from the introduction of the psalmist in 46:1–3: "God is our refuge and strength, a very present help in trouble. Therefore we will not fear, though the earth should change, . . . though its waters roar and foam, though the mountains tremble with its tumult." We recognize in the psalmist's words the promise of help in time of trouble. And like the psalmist, we have confidence—we will get through this, we will survive with God as our help.

Nebuchadnezzar, the king of Babylon, forced Israel into a total rethinking of its understanding of itself in relation to God and the world. The place of that rethinking was exile. The first deportation took place in 597 B.C.E. and had been terribly humiliating. A puppet king of Nebuchadnezzar's liking had been placed on the throne, but all of this was seen as only a blip in Israel's history. Jeremiah had warned the exiles in Babylon to prepare for a long stay: "Build houses and live in them; plant gardens and eat what they produce. Take wives and have sons and daughters; take wives for your sons and give your daughters in marriage, that they may bear sons and daughters; multiply there and do not decrease" (Jeremiah 29:5–6).

The crisis of faith, the loss of the land, the loss of the temple, and the loss of the king raised enormous questions.

> How could we sing the LORD's song
>   in a foreign land?
> If I forget you, O Jerusalem,
>   let my right hand wither!
> Let my tongue cling to the roof of my mouth,
>   if I do not remember you,
>   if I do not set Jerusalem
>   above my highest joy.
>   (Psalm 137:4–6)

We might not recognize the depth of feeling expressed in this psalm until we remember the left hand was never used in social intercourse in the Middle East, only the right hand. It was proffered in fellowship, hospitality, and worship.

The anguish and anger of the closing verses of Psalm 137 may seem difficult to us. But they resonate the despair and the depth of crisis that Israel faced. "Remember, O LORD, against the Edomites the day of Jerusalem's fall, how they said, 'Tear it down! Tear it down! Down to its foundations!' O daughter Babylon, you devastator! Happy shall they be who pay you back what you have done to us! Happy shall they be who take your little ones and dash them against the rock!" (vv. 7–9).

We tend not to use these verses in church because they make us uncomfortable. However, they speak of a reality that we may not want to admit to, but which in our darkest moment we know is present in each of us.

Exile was the place of separation, grief, anger, and darkness. It was also the place where Israel discovered how to speak and think of God as still present in a new way. It was the place where Israel gathered the stories of its sacred history and learned to speak of who it was and why it was.

Throughout our lives we encounter the experience of exile with all that it entails in terms of radical rethinking. However, in the later years of life we all need to come to terms with our mortality and the knowledge that we are not the inviolable creatures that we thought we were. That may be different for each of us, but, one way or another, we recognize the sentiments. We laugh at and make fun of some of the limitations that sometimes, but not always, come with the aging process (vision, hearing, memory, a slowed pace). Some of us greet our own aging with more grace and humor, but none of us can escape it. It means a radical rethinking of who we are and why we are, and we are forced to think of the rest of our lives in a new way.

Some of us want to hang our harps on poplar trees. We get angry when the things that keep us captive and torment us seem to taunt us to sing one of the songs of Zion. We say to ourselves, "Go on and do what you used to do so well—race with friends while biking, charge to the net while playing tennis, run up a mountain, run the marathon—all the things that you did when you were younger, and can't do anymore." We get angry. In the following chapters, some of the experiences, feelings, and issues of aging as seen through the Psalms and the liturgies of life will be explored.

As we have seen in our summary of the historical context in which it was written, Psalm 137 is one of the very special psalms that "comes to life" as it is read in the context of contemporary experience. It speaks of experiences that many people live with daily and struggle with both physically and spiritually. The psalm comes to life for those who have left their native land because of persecution or famine, and have left behind all that is familiar—their friends, their property, their livelihood, and many times, their hopes and dreams for the future. This feeling of being in exile can include those who choose for economic, educational, health, and other personal reasons to become immigrants to a new land to make a new life for themselves—as Koreans, Vietnamese, and others have done in the United States.

Psalm 137 comes to life for older persons who, because of physical limitations, safety, and/or many other reasons, can no longer live independently in the place where they have raised their children, built a lifetime of memories, and where their roots run deep. They must move into smaller quarters, and, for a time, feel like displaced persons who must start over in making friends and building a life. When this happens they know they will never again live in that home place, and even if they did, it would be very different.

The experience of exile can also come when a major transition results in a loss of all that previously gave meaning to life. These transitions include retirement, the death of a spouse, the death of an adult child, or even the loss of a driver's license.

All kinds of emotions emerge in the hearts of people who feel as though they are in exile in a foreign land, for whatever reason. Anger, and sometimes even hatred, emerge against the persons or circumstances that led to the exile. Grief over losses and loved ones left behind, as well as anxiety about the future, only add to the emotional intensity.

It is no wonder that the words of Psalm 137 bring emotional appeal to the reader, of whatever age and in whatever century, because most human beings experience these feelings at some time in their lives, including the later years of life. We may experience a very personal identification with the psalmist when he says: "By the rivers of Babylon—there we sat down and there we wept when we remembered Zion."

WHAT DOES THE PSALM SAY?

Psalm 137

> By the rivers of Babylon—
>   there we sat down and there we wept
>   when we remembered Zion.
> On the willows there
>   we hung up our harps.
> For there our captors
>   asked us for songs,
> and our tormentors asked for mirth, saying,
>   "Sing us one of the songs of Zion!"
> How could we sing the LORD's song
>   in a foreign land?

If I forget you, O Jerusalem,
let my right hand wither!
Let my tongue cling to the roof of my mouth,
if I do not remember you,
if I do not set Jerusalem
above my highest joy.
Remember, O LORD, against the Edomites
the day of Jerusalem's fall,
how they said, "Tear it down! Tear it down!
Down to its foundations!"
O daughter Babylon, you devastator!
Happy shall they be who pay you back
what you have done to us!
Happy shall they be who take your little ones
and dash them against the rock!

Psalm 46

God is our refuge and strength,
a very present help in trouble.
Therefore we will not fear, though the earth should change,
though the mountains shake in the heart of the sea;
though its waters roar and foam,
though the mountains tremble with its tumult.
There is a river whose streams make glad the city of God,
the holy habitation of the Most High.
God is in the midst of the city; it shall not be moved;
God will help it when the morning dawns.
The nations are in an uproar, the kingdoms totter;
he utters his voice, the earth melts.
The LORD of hosts is with us;
the God of Jacob is our refuge.
Come, behold the works of the LORD;
see what desolations he has brought on the earth.
He makes wars cease to the end of the earth;
he breaks the bow, and shatters the spear;
he burns the shields with fire,
"Be still, and know that I am God!
I am exalted among the nations,
I am exalted in the earth."

The LORD of hosts is with us;
the God of Jacob is our refuge.

WHAT DO THESE PSALMS MEAN?

When I think about times in my own life when I have felt as though I were in exile, I think of the many years that I spent serving as a missionary in South Korea, separated from family and everything that was familiar. However, while in Korea, I did not feel as though I were in exile. I cannot call that a time of exile since those were very happy and fulfilling years, and I was in Korea because I felt that God had called me to be there. I wanted to go.

However, I felt as though I were in exile a few years ago when I was diagnosed with breast cancer twice and had two mastectomies, all within twelve months. I was in a place where I did not want to be. This was entirely new and strange territory. I was fearful, angry, and felt very much alone.

Even though I was surrounded by caring friends and family, I did not choose to be there, and I knew my life would never be the same again. My world had changed, and so had I. I could no longer feel invincible as I had in previous years. I knew that I would spend the rest of my life going to doctors to ascertain whether or not the "enemy" had returned. My "temple," as I had known it, was destroyed. So, in that place of desolation and aloneness "there I sat down and there I wept." For a time I could not bring myself to sing the Lord's song in that strange and foreign land. It took some months for me to rebuild my life from the experience of exile, and to realize that although life could never be the same, there was life after exile.

The themes in Psalm 137 speak of these feelings—remembering what was lost, grieving over and adjusting to the loss, and expressing anger. Psalm 137 is a lament concerning the destruction of Jerusalem, filled with expressions of bitter memories and deep pain over loss. It focuses on two cities—Babylon, against which there was great anger and resistance, and Jerusalem, a place beloved and remembered with deep passion.

Psalm 137 has three emphases: First, the people in exile speak of their grief as they remember Jerusalem and their humiliation as they are taunted by their captors. Second, they vow their faithfulness and that they will never forget their homeland. Third, the writer of the psalm petitions the Lord to respond directly to what has happened to Israel by bringing retribution against Babylon. Their prayer is an appeal for vindication: "Happy shall they be who pay you back what you have done to us!" (v. 8).

The demand of the tormentors, "Sing us one of the songs of Zion!" (v. 3), is reminiscent of Psalm 42:3 when the psalmist was asked, "Where is your God?" The implication is now that Jerusalem is in ruins. "Tell us now about your all-powerful God!" The psalmist has such strong feelings about what has happened to Jerusalem, and is so passionate concerning his remembering the experience of loss, he exaggerates greatly in order to make his point: "Let my right hand wither! Let my tongue cling to the roof of my mouth" (137:5–6).

Then we come to the verse that is so difficult: "Happy shall they be who take your little ones and dash them against the rock!" (v. 9). This obviously comes out of deep anger, asking that a terrible wrong be answered by another terrible wrong. Some scholars indicate that the slaughter of children was a military procedure used occasionally in order to eliminate a population, similar to present-day "ethnic cleansing." However, as Mays points out, this does not come out of a personal desire for savage revenge, but "out of a zeal for the Lord and the place of the Lord's habitation."[2]

Anger is an emotion found throughout the scriptures. There is human anger against God, God's anger against humans, human anger against other humans, and human anger against events in life. Since anger is such a prevalent emotion in scripture, perhaps it has more importance than is given to it in the modern world. Anger in Psalm 137, as a part of the grief experienced, comes full force in verses 8–9 calling on God for revenge.

The Interpreter's Dictionary of the Bible offers some insights about biblical anger that may be helpful in your consideration of the subject of anger in Psalm 137:

> In the OT [Old Testament] one finds a qualified justification of anger insofar as it operates in the service of faith and piety, in the defense of justice generally or in

particular in the condemnation of violations of God's claims to sovereignty [see 2 Samuel 12:5–7, and Exodus 16:20].

The wisdom sages explicitly condemn anger as antithetical to [shalom] in that it stirs up trouble and has harmful consequences [see Proverbs 6:34].

In spite of some concessions in the NT [New Testament] regarding human anger, it seems to be the general view there that "the anger of man does not work the righteousness of God" [see James 1:19–20]. The admonition of the writer of Ephesians to "be angry but do not sin" (4:26) is scarcely a commendation of anger to man but a warning that anger provides exceptional opportunity for sinful self-elevation and overt trespasses.[3]

Walter Brueggemann points out that "the speaker does not, in fact, crush the heads of babes against rocks. It is a prayer, a wish, a hope, a yearning. . . . At first glance, Psalm 137 strikes us as a childish outburst. On reflection, it may be the voice of seasoned religion that knows profoundly what it costs to beat off despair. More than simply knowing the cost, this speaker is prepared to pay." Brueggemann further comments that "it is an act of profound faith to entrust one's most precious hatreds to God, knowing they will be taken seriously."[4]

It must also be remembered that out of the ashes of Jerusalem there arose a New Jerusalem. Out of the anger and resentment of the people written about by the psalmist, newness emerged. There are examples of this newness in the modern world. When African American churches have been burned to the ground out of racial hatred, in most cases new churches have arisen, more alive, more beautiful, and more compassionate than ever before.

The New Interpreter's Bible says of anger, "One thing it teaches us, for instance, is the lesson that in extreme situations, grief and anger are both inevitable and inseparable. The worst possible response to monstrous evil is to feel nothing. In the absence of these feelings, evil becomes an acceptable commonplace. . . . [T]o forget is to submit to evil, to wither and die; to remember is to resist, to be faithful, and to live again."[5]

Some questions to consider concerning Psalm 137 are:

1. What place does anger have in human life and in human relationships with God?

2. Is there such a thing as godly anger?

3. Describe healthy and unhealthy ways of handling anger.

4. How can a person deal with anger in a pastoral and spiritual manner?

5. Is revenge ever a good response to persons who have caused you pain? Why or why not?

6. What is the appropriate way in which to deal with hurts and resentments from the distant past?

7. What does this psalm teach about relating to other persons who have experienced losses and feel as though they are in "exile"?

8. Older people are sometimes accused of hanging on to the past, of retaining the hatreds of their childhood and allowing resentments of the past to determine their future relationships. What does this psalm say, if anything, about hanging on to past memories?

Psalm 46 comes rushing forth with what is perhaps the most powerful statement of faith and assurance in the whole of the Psalms. This is especially true for persons in exile, who face devastating losses and a hopeless future. Rather than focusing on the losses, the writer finds comfort and joy in emphasizing who God is and what God has done. As *The New Interpreter's Bible* observes, "it is fundamentally an affirmation of faith—not in Zion, but in God."[6]

The power of Psalm 46 is evident in the words used to describe God: *refuge, strength,* and *help. The Oxford Dictionary of Current English* defines *refuge* as "shelter from pursuit, danger, or trouble." If you have been chased by someone in the midst of road rage, or if you have been in a severe thunderstorm or hurricane, or if you have been in some other kind of chaotic situation, think how these words would feel to you: "God is our refuge and strength, a very present help in trouble" (v. 1).

On the farm where my grandparents lived, and where I visited often during my growing up years, there was a storm cellar in which to take refuge if a hurricane or violent storm came. During World War II there were bomb shelters to provide refuge for people in case of falling bombs. To see God as *refuge* means safety and security. God has the *strength* (God's sovereignty) to provide the *help* needed.

Verses 4–7 provide support and confirmation for the first three verses of Psalm 46. Although there is no river in Jerusalem, the phrase in verse 4, "there is a river whose streams make glad the city of God," is metaphorical. The phrase indicates that the river provides sustenance for life. The river becomes a life-giving stream. When everything is in an uproar, when the powers who rule are tottering, and when everything around is unstable, the psalmist says, "Don't worry! What really counts is that God is stable, and you can count on God." Even in the worst-case scenarios of verses 2 and 3, "there is a river . . . "!

Then there come some imperatives, some verbs, to *come* and *see* for yourself what God has done and is doing. Look at the list of what God has done: God makes wars cease, bows to break, spears to shatter, and shields to burn. Therefore, the result is the final imperative, "Be still, and know that I am God!" (v. 10).

The New Interpreter's Bible puts a different twist on this verse. It points out that the translation for "be still" is not a good translation, but is used because it is familiar. When we read the words "be still," we think that we need to relax, think godly thoughts, pray, or meditate. However, a closer translation might be something like, "Stop!" or "Throw down your weapons!" "In other words, 'Depend upon God instead of yourselves.'"[7]

In his book *A Theological Introduction to the Book of Psalms,* J. Clinton McCann Jr. points out that "we have tanks and submarines and nuclear warheads and 'smart bombs' and patriot missiles, known as 'Peacekeepers,'" demonstrating what we depend upon for our security. But Psalm 46 states clearly that real security and real peace do not come from human efforts or what we can produce in the way of "peacekeeping" equipment. McCann goes on to suggest that it doesn't matter what happens, even nuclear holocaust, for "God will prevail."[8]

Some questions to ponder concerning Psalm 46 are:

1. What difference would it make if we chose other options for seeking peace rather than tanks, submarines, nuclear warheads, etc.? Why do we not look at other options?
2. If we chose the option suggested in Psalm 46, to "Be still,

and know that I am God," what would that mean for us as a nation in seeking peace in the world?

3. "A very present help in trouble" is a beautiful, almost poetic, expression. What does it really mean?

PUTTING IT ALL TOGETHER AND BRINGING IT HOME

1. What is your own personal Jerusalem?
2. What is your Babylon? What are your "rivers of Babylon"?
3. By what measure do you determine your happiness or unhappiness?
4. Identify in your mind a personal experience of being exiled and describe how that felt to you.
5. To what do you promise faithfulness when you are feeling lost or in despair?
6. What is your greatest fear?
7. What image comes to mind when you remember God's faithfulness to you during your life? Where are you aware of God's faithfulness in your life ?
8. How do you handle anger in your life?
9. When you perceive that the whole world is in chaos, and in addition to that, your own personal world is also out of control, how can this psalm be helpful to you?
10. If God "makes wars to cease, breaks the bow, shatters the spear and burns the shields with fire," what are we missing in today's world? Is this a power, a sovereignty that we are missing? Is this a dream world the psalmist is writing about? What is going on here?

HELPS FOR GROUP STUDY

A. Begin the session by dividing the participants into three groups for reading Psalm 137 in unison. Ask group 1 to read verses 1–3, group 2 to read verses 4–6, and group 3 to read verses 7–9. When this is complete, ask for volunteers to read Psalm 137 again, one verse at a time, from different translations until all persons who wish to read have had the opportunity to do so.

This may mean repeating the psalm a few times. Identify the differences in translation and discuss whether or not the different translations give different meanings to the verses.

B. Ask the group to identify the key words, images, and phrases found in Psalm 137, such as "Sing us one of the songs of Zion!" (v. 3), "Let my right hand wither!" (v. 5), and "Happy shall they be who pay you back what you have done to us!" (v. 8). Why are these words, images, and phrases important? What others seem significant to you and why?

C. Ask the group the following questions of Psalm 137:
   1. In verses 1–3, what is the dominant feeling expressed?
   2. In verses 4–6, what is the message of the psalmist to the readers?
   3. In verses 7–9, what is the main emotion shown, and why?

D. Discuss what the group believes to be the message the psalmist is trying to communicate.

E. Ask the group to identify the theological and personal issues raised by the psalm by asking the following:
   1. How would you describe a "theology of anger"?
   2. Is it "theologically correct" to pray for revenge against those who have caused you pain?
   3. The psalmist, in the midst of feelings of grief and loss, pledges to be faithful to his memory of Jerusalem. Further, he indicates that he will pray for terrible things to happen if the exiles should get comfortable in the new situation and forget Jerusalem. What does the psalmist fear?
   4. What are the theological implications of the psalmist wishing all manner of horrible things for those who caused the losses?
   5. What is the theological implication of a new Jerusalem rising from the ashes?
   6. What might be the message of the psalm to the modern world? To the participants in the group?

F. Discuss the meaning of anger in the scriptures. Is it good or bad?

G. Ask the group to read Psalm 46 and to identify the most significant words, phrases, and images used. This psalm can also be used effectively as a responsive reading with the group if all have the same translation.

H. Discuss the following questions based on Psalm 46:
1. How is God our refuge, strength, and help?
2. When all around us is in chaos, how can we latch onto "a very present help in trouble"?
3. What is the difference in purpose between corporate worship and individual worship? How can corporate worship be helpful to an individual who is in anguish, fear, and anger? How can individual worship be helpful to such an individual?
4. How does Psalm 46 become a word of grace, a "very present help"?

Notes

1. James L. Mays, *Psalms,* Interpretation: A Bible Commentary for Teaching and Preaching (Louisville, Ky.: John Knox Press, 1994), 185.
2. Ibid., 423.
3. "Anger," *The Interpreter's Dictionary of the Bible,* vol. 1 (Nashville: Abingdon Press, 1962), 136.
4. Walter Brueggemann, *The Message of the Psalms: A Theological Commentary,* Old Testament Studies (Minneapolis: Augsburg Publishing House, 1984), 77.
5. *The New Interpreter's Bible,* vol. 4 (Nashville: Abingdon Press, 1996), 1228.
6. Ibid., 864.
7. Ibid., 866.
8. J. Clinton McCann Jr., *A Theological Introduction to the Book of Psalms* (Nashville: Abingdon Press, 1993), 140.

Suggestions for Further Reading

Best, Robert J., and Jackqueline A. Brunner. *Memories of Home: A Keepsake You Create.* Mahwah, N.J.: Paulist Press, 1994.

Morgan, Richard L. *With Faces to the Evening Sun.* Nashville: Upper Room Books, 1998.

Chapter 3

Psalm 8
WHO AM I? WHAT IS
MY PLACE IN ALL OF THIS?

*The Psalms can help us give voice to the anguish
and the lostness. . . . They represent a vibrant
and compelling call to remember and to celebrate
the involvement of God in sacred history, by telling
the stories over and over again.*
—Elizabeth J. Canham

INTRODUCTION

At Christmas time I play a tape of music with strong spiritual leanings, Barbra Streisand's *Higher Ground*. The last track is powerful. Sung in Hebrew is the prayer of Rosh Hashanah, or Avinu Malkeinu, the Jewish New Year. It is a prayer of confession to God asking for compassion, and a plea to God to help us bring an end to pestilence, war, and famine. The final three lines are penetrating: "Cause all hate and oppression to vanish from the earth; Inscribe us for blessing in the Book Of Life, Let the new year be a good year for us."

Many scholars think Psalm 8 belongs to the festival of the new year. Of course, the cosmology of the psalmist is vastly different from that of our own. The psalmist lived in a world in which the earth was the center of the universe and the sun moved around it. High above the flat earth was a dome, the heavens, and above the heavens dwelt the Holy One of Israel. At the center of the earth was the human being, to whom God gave dominion over the rest of creation. Human beings were the crowning glory.

This view of cosmology is clearly reflected in Psalm 8. The sovereignty of God above the heavens is declared in verse 1: "O LORD, our Lord, how majestic is your name in all the earth! You have set your glory above the heavens" (NIV). *The New Interpreter's Bible* indicates that Psalm 8 had the distinction of being the first biblical text to reach the moon, having been included in a silicon disc made up of messages from seventy-three nations, and left on the moon by Apollo 11 in 1969. Further, it is said that Psalm 8 was an appropriate choice for this occasion, for "it is both an eloquent proclamation of the cosmic sovereignty of God and a remarkable affirmation of the exalted status and vocation of the human creature."[1]

Human beings appear to be unique in the created order. Whether it is because we are God's final crowning glory in creation or because of the God-inspired evolutionary process is a much-debated question. However, in a sense, origins don't matter. We have come to realize what the psalmist grasped very forcefully—that humankind is part of God's created order, which includes the earth and all that dwells therein, the skies and universes yet to be discovered. In recent years, our connectedness to earth and the fragile balance of nature has been brought to our attention by way of environmental concerns. Most of the time, our lifestyles are in conflict with these concerns. We have yet to digest the full meaning of the wisdom of one of our North American ancestors. In "A Letter to the Great White Chief in Washington," Chief Seattle (1786–1866) wrote, "This earth does not belong to us, we belong to the earth. . . . All things are connected like the blood which unites one family. . . . We do not weave the web of life, we are only a strand in it. Whatever we do to the web, we do to ourselves."[2]

The psalmist's worldview is vastly different from our own, yet the questions asked remain basic for humankind through the ages. Who am I? What am I? What is my place? These are human questions, no matter what our age.

After serving as chaplain in a large retirement community in Atlanta, I became chaplain at Agnes Scott College in Decatur. I discovered that the students were dealing with some of the same issues as the residents in the retirement community—identity, changing family relationships, and low self-esteem. Both groups were asking, "Who am I now in my present circumstance, now that my family relationships have changed, now that I am in a place of transition in my life?" I have chosen Psalm 8 for study because it speaks to the older adult issues of self-esteem, identity, and one's role in the world.

In the movie, *On Golden Pond,* these two ages of humankind were vividly contrasted. An older couple, Norman and Ethel Thayer (played by Henry Fonda and Katharine Hepburn) are spending their forty-eighth summer at their cabin by a lake. Their daughter, Chelsea (played by Jane Fonda), her fiancé (played by Dabney Coleman), and his teenage son, Billy (played by Doug McKeon) come to the lake to visit Chelsea's parents. After a short visit, Chelsea and her fiancé depart for a trip to Europe, leaving Billy at the lake with the older couple. At the beginning of his time at the lake, tempers flare, teenage rebellion runs rampant, and relationships are tense. The young boy is struggling to find his place in a world of changing relationships and his own emerging identity. At the same time, this is contrasted with the older adult, Norman, whose identity had always been his professional work life. Now he feels as if there is no direction in his life. This is evident when Norman goes out to pick berries and becomes lost, disoriented, and frightened as he wanders around in the woods trying to find his way back home in surroundings that used to be so familiar to him. Eventually, Norman has a serious clash with Billy, and unfairly blames Billy for something he himself had done. Ethel, trying very hard to help both Norman and Billy through their struggles, says to Billy, "Don't be too hard on Norman. He is just trying to find his way through, just like you." Both old and young are dealing with the same issues of who they are in these new relationships and new circumstances.

"What is man that thou art mindful of him?" What does this conjure up for us? First of all, for some it may bring to mind that since "man" is used in the RSV and the NIV, this question has nothing to do with women. Since the psalmist was writing within a patriarchal framework, it is more than likely that the psalmist did indeed have in mind the male human being. Rule and responsibility at that time were given to men. As we enter a new millennium, the male is still seen as the more authoritative sex in most places in the world, including the United States. His identity is still tied up with that worldview even now, although to a lesser extent than in previous times. For instance, when talking with a man at a party, the first sentences in the conversation are frequently about where he works. A woman will usually refer to herself in relation to her husband or her children if she is married and/or has children, or her parents if she is not. Many times her response has nothing to do with who she really is herself. Thankfully, this is changing. However, women traditionally have been into relationships and men into work identity, and there is some residue from this view that remains with us.

In writing about the word *man,* Robert Alter says that the "Hebrew etymological pun is Adam, humus, from the soil," and that it does not mean a male human being at all.[3] In other words, the Hebrew concept was about being connected to the created order, not about gender. The NRSV translation is more inclusive: "What are human beings that you are mindful of them, mortals that you care for them?" (v. 4).

The psalmist is focusing on the tremendous idea that we are on the mind of God. The American Standard Version translates the text as "what is man that thou art mindful of him, and the son of man that thou visitest him?" The New International Version has, "that you care for him." We have the enviable position of being in the mind of God. Our task then is to work out who we are, knowing that we are on the mind of God.

The important issue for the psalmist was, Who am I in connection with all that is around me? If I am connected with all of creation, what is my place in the whole scheme of things? Where do I fit in? "The identity of humanity cannot be understood apart from this relationship with God."[4]

The Hebrew people of biblical times were called by God as a community. If you were not in a community, you did not exist. So the drive was to work it out, whatever it was, in community, not as mere self-gratification. The source of self-worth is what the psalmist is asking about: Who am I in relationship to community and to the created order? The psalmist is not referring at all to the individual.

This runs counter to everything in our modern world, with our hang-ups concerning being independent and developing our own individuality. It runs counter to how we view success and productivity, as well as the satisfaction of our consumer desires.

Some older adults are simply trying to survive economically, and these questions are a luxury. However, in this country many are dealing with these issues and asking these questions.

In addition to addressing the issue of identity, Psalm 8 speaks to one of the most basic needs of all human beings, the need for feelings of self-worth. The need for self-esteem has been identified as particularly important in the lives of older adults who are no longer in the mainstream of society where productivity, as society defines productivity, is the major gauge for measuring human worth. Psalm 8 points to the true source of human worth—the Creator God in relationship with the created order. Arnold B. Rhodes has called this psalm "Genesis 1 set to music."[5] This psalm is indeed closely related to the creation story in Genesis, and raises two inseparably related questions: Who is God? And who are human beings in God's creation?

The psalm goes further and looks behind the beauty of creation to ponder the nature of the one who created it, with only the thought of praise as the basic motivation and intention. Both the beginning and the end of the psalm give expression to this thought. In between, however, the place given to human beings in creation speaks to this basic human need for self-worth. The psalm speaks both to the insignificance of human beings and, at the same time, of the high value and trust that God places in human life and participation in the created world.

The questions to be explored, then, are: By observing nature what can human beings learn about themselves? What can they know about God? Is it possible for older adults who are retired and who are sitting on the sidelines of the mainstream of society to lay claim to the kind of self-worth described in the psalm? What is the message of Psalm 8 to older adults today? What about older adults who are busier than they have ever been before—traveling to intriguing places, volunteering their time and talents in all kinds of ways, caring for grandchildren, and caring for older family members? Can they also lay claim to the self-worth described in the psalm? With these questions in mind, read Psalm 8. Use of the New Revised Standard Version (NRSV) is suggested because of its more inclusive rendition of the text.

WHAT DOES THE PSALM SAY?

Psalm 8

> O LORD, our Sovereign,
>> how majestic is your name in all the earth!
>
> You have set your glory above the heavens.
>> Out of the mouths of babes and infants
>
> you have founded a bulwark because of your foes,
>> to silence the enemy and the avenger.
>
> When I look at your heavens, the work of your fingers,
>> the moon and the stars that you have established;
>
> what are human beings that you are mindful of them,
>> mortals that you care for them?
>
> Yet you have made them a little lower than God [or, than
>> the divine beings or angels],
>
> and crowned them with glory and honor.
>
> You have given them dominion over the works of your
>> hands;
>
> you have put all things under their feet,
>
> all sheep and oxen,
>> and also the beasts of the field,
>
> the birds of the air, and the fish of the sea,
>> whatever passes along the paths of the seas.
>
> O LORD, our Sovereign,
>> how majestic is your name in all the earth!

As background study for Psalm 8, read the creation stories in Genesis (Genesis 1:1–2:3 and 2:4–25). Walter Brueggemann observes that "as the Bible starts with a line of defense against chaos, so our understanding of the Psalms begins with a celebration of good order. In both texts, humanity stands at the crucial center of that good order."[6]

What message do you think the psalmist had in mind for those who would sing or hear this hymn? You may want to explore how the psalmist puts together the two concepts found in the psalm—the worth of human beings and the insignificance of human beings—at the same time, how the vastness and beauty of God's creation brings forth praise, the unbelievable trust that God has placed in creation, and the interrelatedness of God with creation, especially with human beings. In this psalm, what glimpses do you get of God's purposes in creating the world and placing human beings in it?

WHAT DOES THE PSALM MEAN?

A look at the historical context of Psalm 8 is helpful. Although the psalm is entitled "A Psalm of David," it is not certain whether David actually wrote the psalm, or whether the caption simply means that the psalm was part of a collection of psalms written to David, according to David, or in honor of David. Traditionally, David is accepted as the author. There is no indication within the psalm of a date or a time during which it may have been written.

However, there are some internal clues as to where and what time of day it was sung. Since the psalmist mentions the moon and the stars, it may have been written at night. The psalm is a mixture of corporate praise, as in "our LORD" (vv. 1 and 9), and individual confession and teaching: "When I look at the heavens . . . " (vv. 3–8). It is likely that the setting for the psalm was one of the evening celebrations in the temple courts of Jerusalem, perhaps at one of the festivals. Hans-Ruedi Weber suggests it may have been a New Year's celebration that had in it a service of praise centered around the greatness of the Creator and the creation.[7]

Some of the words and phrases in Psalm 8 need further exploration in order to interpret the message of the psalm. For example:

1. "O LORD, our Lord" (v. 1), although translated the same in English, come from two different Hebrew words. The first word translated as "LORD" is *Yahweh,* which was for Israel the proper name of God. Although the original meaning of the word is not certain, it is important in its historical associations, particularly what God said to Moses on Mount Sinai: "I am the LORD [Yahweh] your God, who brought you out of the land of Egypt, out of the house of slavery" (Exodus 20:2). The meaning had to do with how Yahweh revealed the divine name and character through mighty deeds in the lives of human beings. The second "Lord" in the verse is *Adonai.* It was an honorific title, simply meaning "your honor," indicating the bearer's position and authority. However, according to *The Interpreter's Dictionary of the*

Bible, later the word began to include not just honor and respect, but also an expression of God's absolute lordship.[8]

Therefore, *Yahweh* carries with it the whole tradition of the covenant relationship of God with human beings, of the promise of presence, and of the sustaining of human beings through their difficult times, especially of transition and of being uprooted from all that is familiar. *Adonai* carries with it the idea of standing in awe of God, of showing honor and respect, and also of claiming God's sovereignty over all.

2. "Out of the mouths of babes and infants you have founded a bulwark because of your foes, to silence the enemy and the avenger" (v. 2). This is the most difficult phrase in the psalm to translate and to be understood. The Hebrew is unclear and the concept difficult to grasp. There are many interpretations given by various scholars. The reason for this is a textual problem in the beginning of the verse that cannot be resolved with certainty. Some interpretations indicate that these verses have to do with God using the poor and the weak to accomplish God's work, that the enemies of God are human beings who fight against God's purposes. This interpretation indicates that through the frail, the weak, and the insignificant—such as babes and children—God confronts the enemies. This is consistent with the rest of the psalm as it compares the greatness of God with the insignificance of human beings. This is certainly a projection, and the meaning that the psalmist had in mind remains a mystery. Eugene Peterson's paraphrase offers a possible meaning: "Nursing infants gurgle choruses about you; toddlers shout the songs that drown out enemy talk and silence atheist babble."[9] This verse is reflected in the New Testament Gospel of Mark: "Whoever does not receive the kingdom of God as a little child will never enter it" (10:15).

Others suggest these verses are about the innocence of children and their awe in looking at creation. Think about children as they are discovering the world around them. They look around, see creation, and say, "Wow! Look at that bird!" or "Wow! Look at those flowers!" The focus, according to some, is innocence, like Jesus putting a child in the midst of his audience and saying, "You must be like this." At what point in our lives do we stop noticing and wondering with wide eyes the magic of the firefly? Ideally, we never do. The challenge of the older adult years is to retain the wonder of the created world. Is it still possible for me to look at the world and wonder? It is easy to get self-absorbed in everyday living, in health problems, in just getting by, when there is the whole world out there to explore!

3. "Little lower than God" (v. 5a) also has varied interpretations. *God* here is sometimes translated "angels," as in the King James Version, or "a god," as in the Jerusalem Bible. This represents a third word in the Hebrew language for God in the same psalm—*Elohim*. The word *Elohim* sometimes refers to the whole company of God. The word was changed to "angels" in the Greek Septuagint translation and this is how it appears when the verse is quoted in the New Testament Letter to the Hebrews (2:6–8). The context would seem to indicate that *angels* fits better since the point being made is of the infinite greatness of God and the comparative insignificance of human beings.[10] But here too the meaning of the psalm remains hidden in the text. A possible meaning is that in comparison to God's whole creation humans are insignificant. Yet God has put humans in charge of it all. Could we also say that when we older adults are viewed by society as insignificant, God is expecting great things of us?

4. "You have given them dominion" (v. 6) points to the other side of the relationship with God. Human beings have been seen by the psalmist as insignificant in comparison to the greatness of creation, but in view of the trust that God has exhibited by giving human beings this vocation, the value and the worth of human beings has been raised above all other parts of creation.

WHAT DIFFERENCE DOES IT MAKE?

Some theological issues that arise from a discussion of Psalm 8 are:

1. What kind of God is experienced in Psalm 8? What does the psalm teach us about God? Think of some adjectives that the reader of Psalm 8 might use to describe God.

2. If the psalmist is saying that God works through the weak and the poor more than through the rich and the powerful, what difference would that make in how human beings think about themselves and God? What difference would it make in how we order our lives?

3. If the interpretation of verse 2 has to do with looking at creation and saying, "Wow!" how can we hold on to these childhood feelings of awe as we view the beauty and vastness of God's creation?

4. What does the psalm teach about the worth of human beings? What difference could this psalm make in how we think of ourselves?

5. What does the psalm teach about the interrelatedness between God and God's creation, especially human beings? If we accepted this interrelatedness, what difference could it make?

The reading of Psalm 8 also raises some questions concerning personal issues:

1. The psalmist indicates that human beings have two tasks: the praise of God (v. 1), and stewardship over the earth (v. 6). In other words, worship and work go together. What happens to the rhythm of work and worship when a person retires, or because of physical limitations can no longer work?

2. The psalmist is moved to praise when he views the beauty of creation. Experience tells us that when viewing a beautiful sunset or the moon and the stars on a clear night, praise can come naturally and easily. What about when one is viewing the ugly, hurtful side of humanity? How does one praise God in the midst of injustice, hunger, violence, despair, anger, or physical illness?

3. The psalmist paints a picture of human beings as a little lower than "God" or "the angels," but as having "dominion over the works of your hands." We have worth because we were created by God and given a vocation by God, according to the psalmist. If we truly accept this view, what difference could it make in our lives, in our nation, and in the world?

PUTTING IT ALL TOGETHER
AND BRINGING IT HOME

In order to focus the various themes set forth by the psalmist in relationship to your own personal day-to-day living, it might be helpful to reflect upon these questions:

1. What issues or themes in Psalm 8 most closely touch your own struggles at the present time?
2. What is the central message of Psalm 8 for us in our present circumstances?
3. With which verses do you most easily identify? What are they saying to you?

It may well be that the most significant message of the psalm is that the psalmist gives the reader an important perspective for life. The psalmist points to who God is, who human beings are in relationship to God, and who human beings are in relation to the rest of creation. If these perspectives could be claimed, problems of self-worth (either too much or too little) and problems of identity as persons or roles in life would seem to diminish. It may be that when the perspective is distorted, feelings of uselessness and low self-esteem emerge. But in this psalm the reader gets a clear signal of who human beings are in God's plan for the world, and what we are called to do and to be.

HELPS FOR GROUP STUDY

A. Begin the session by reading Psalm 8 from the Good News Bible. Then ask group members to read it again, one verse at a time from the various translations, with special attention given to verses 2 and 5a. Compare the translations and discuss the significance of the differences.

B. Review the creation stories in Genesis (1:1–2:3 and 2:4–25). Discuss some or all of the following questions:
   1. What is the element of time stated?
   2. What is the location or place of creation?
   3. When in the process were human beings created?
   4. When in the process was woman created?
   5. What is the relationship between the created order and God?
   6. What is the relationship of humankind to the rest of creation?
   7. What is the essential message of the passage in Genesis?

C. Discuss these questions concerning the writing of the

psalm itself: What seems to have been going on in the life of the psalmist when he wrote Psalm 8? What was the occasion for the writing of it?

D. Identify the key words, images, or phrases that give a clue to the message of the psalm, such as "O LORD, our Lord" (v. 1), "babes and infants" (v. 2), "little lower than God" (v. 5), "dominion over the works of your hands" (v. 6).

E. Ask group members to explore what they believe the psalmist to be saying to the people of his day. Some questions to ponder include:

1. How can you put together the image of God as a personal God with whom we have a personal relationship, and the belief that God is also "our Lord," the God of the community of believers. How can both be reflected in order that true worship can take place?

2. Does God show power by choosing to use the weak to bring a message to the powerful? If so, does that work?

3. We believe that God shows power by choosing to entrust the whole of God's creation into the hands of human beings. Does this not limit God's power by placing human beings in charge of things?

4. How do you see the paradox presented here, that human beings are insignificant when compared to God's creation and yet are given significance and worth, a lifetime vocation, and the opportunity to be in relationship with the Creator?

5. Is the message for older adults living in the twentieth century different from the message to the psalmist's first readers? If not, why not? If so, in what way?

F. Ask group members to think back on their experiences and to choose a story to share concerning when they felt most like the psalmist must have felt as he gazed at the moon and the stars. This could be any event—an awesome experience, a breathtaking view of nature, or some other experience that brought forth the feelings of awesomeness before God and the insignificance of human beings.

G. Ask the group: When have you felt the nearest to having full control of your life? Think of a time when you felt completely out of control, as though you had no control over your life. In view of these experiences, what does it mean that God has given human beings dominion over all things?

H. Ask those who are retired to think about how it felt to leave the work world, and what they did at that point to maintain their feelings of self-esteem and usefulness to society. Ask those who are not retired to think of friends and family members who have retired, and reflect upon what they did to maintain their self-esteem.

I. Invite the group to respond to the study of Psalm 8 in a meaningful way. For example, some might like to write their own psalm based on their own circumstances and experiences. Others might choose to respond by being a friend to someone who is lonely, by reading to someone with failing vision, or by finding some other way of being helpful and supportive to other persons.

Notes

1. *The New Interpreter's Bible,* vol. 4 (Nashville: Abingdon Press, 1996), 711.

2. There is uncertainty about the origin of this excerpt attributed to Chief Seattle. Tradition says that it came from an address by Chief Seattle of the Suquamish and Duwamish tribes at an assembly before white settlers in 1854. It was published in a Seattle newspaper some years later, perhaps as many as thirty years later. However, it has been used throughout the years and accepted as coming from Chief Seattle by Native American groups who say it represents Native American beliefs both then and now.

3. Robert Alter, *Translation and Commentary on Genesis* (New York: W. W. Norton & Co., 1996), 8.

4. *New Interpreter's Bible,* 4:711.

5. Arnold B. Rhodes, *Psalms,* The Layman's Bible Commentary (Atlanta: John Knox Press, 1960), 35.

6. Walter Brueggemann, *The Message of the Psalms: A Theological Commentary,* Old Testament Studies (Minneapolis: Augsburg Publishing House, 1984), 37.

7. Hans-Ruedi Weber, *Experiments with Bible Study* (Philadelphia: Westminster Press, 1981), 62.

8. "Names of God," *The Interpreter's Dictionary of the Bible* (Nashville: Abingdon Press, 1962), 414.

9. Eugene H. Peterson, *The Message: Psalms* (Colorado Springs: Nav Press, 1994), 17.

10. A. A. Anderson, *Psalms,* The New Century Bible Commentary, vol. 1 (Grand Rapids: Wm. B. Eerdmans Publishing Co. and London: Marshall, Morgan & Scott Publishing, 1972), 704.

Chapter 4

Psalms 102 and 103
LIVING ON LIFE'S
ROLLER COASTER

The book of Psalms provides the most reliable theological, pastoral, and liturgical resource given us in the biblical tradition. In season and out of season, generation after generation, faithful women and men turn to the Psalms as a most helpful resource for conversation with God about things that matter most.

—Walter Brueggemann

INTRODUCTION

I am a reluctant aunt, especially when it comes to roller coasters. This became apparent when I went with my fourteen-year-old nephew to Six Flags over Georgia in Atlanta several years ago. All day Todd begged me to ride the roller coaster with him. All day I resisted, until just before time to return home. I realized that if I did not have that pinnacle experience with him, he would never let me forget it. So we boarded the roller coaster. It was up and down, twisting and turning, upside down and downside up, racing toward what I felt to be sure death. It was all right going up the inclines, just slowly chugging along. It even could be boring, if anticipation of what was coming did not overshadow it. Suddenly, flying down the slope I was absolutely sure that I would not survive when we hit the bottom. But I did survive. I was thankful that it was over and that I had made my nephew very happy. I am not sure what he reveled in most, that I rode it with him or that I was scared out of my wits. After that experience I vowed to myself that I would never, ever, ride a roller coaster again. I think the reason I made that vow is that riding that roller coaster is too much like real life. Slow on the uptake, a little boring at times, but when the difficulties come on the downside survival is not in the picture.

This is the image that comes to mind for Psalms 102 and 103. We live in a world that can bring chaos to our lives, change to our routines, distress to our serenity, loneliness to our hearts, and illness to our bodies. At the same time, we live in a world that provides vast opportunities for the enjoyment of life, enrichment to the soul, challenges to the mind, and joy for the whole being. Most of the time we live in between the two, moving from the heights of ecstasy to the depths of despair and back again. Joy and satisfaction come frequently, and so do the experiences of loss, grief, and despair. The psalmist goes from "I am like a lonely bird on the housetop" in Psalm 102:7 to "Bless the LORD, O my soul, and all that is within me, bless his holy name" in Psalm 103:1. The question arises, How does the psalmist move from the deepest despair to the heights of blissful living within a few verses?

These two psalms depict the roller coaster image of life. Although there seems to be no evidence that they were originally one psalm, for purposes of this study we will treat the two psalms together.

Psalm 102 is a psalm of lament, filled with anguish, suffering, feelings of persecution, isolation, and loneliness. Psalm 103 is a psalm of praise, enumerating all the ways in which God has blessed the psalmist. It begins with a beautiful expression of an individual's deep sense of gratitude to God for the forgiveness of sins, for recovery from a serious illness, and for putting life back together again. This image of the roller coaster is not unique to these two psalms, but is a theme that runs throughout the writings of the ancient hymn writers. Psalms 22–24 take the reader from "My God, my God, why have you forsaken me?" in Psalm 22:1 to "The LORD is my shepherd, I shall not want" in Psalm 23:1 to "Lift up your heads, O gates! and be lifted up, O ancient doors! that the King of glory may come in" in Psalm 24:7. We have this kind of "up and down" experience constantly in our own lives, and so in our study of these psalms we will explore how the psalmist lives on the roller coaster of life, and then is able to express gratitude and praise to God for it.

The first half of Psalm 102 is about finitude, about the passing of time: "My days pass away like smoke" (v. 3). The people in exile were very aware of finitude, but had thought before the exile that they had all the time in the world. We are like that. We think all is well and all will be well, and then something happens that shows us how little control we have over time. The psalmist says it this way: "My days are like an evening shadow" (v. 11).

The second half of Psalm 102 is about the totally different nature of God concerning time. As James Mays writes, "With the Lord time is a matter, not of days, but of years, and generations and forever."[1] The psalmist is longing for the restoration of Zion. He has moved on from "How could we sing the LORD's song in a foreign land?"(137:4), which expresses shock that the exile happened, to "But you, O LORD, are enthroned forever; your name endures to all generations" (102:12). The anger has dissipated and there is despair, but also the underlying belief that God will restore Zion. God will build again from the ruins, and the people in exile shall return. Then Psalm 103 rushes in with praise and thanksgiving, as though the restoration and return have already happened.

The reality of the return to the temple was very, very different. Zion had been rebuilt, but the people looked at it and wept. They remembered that the one before was so much better; this temple was not like Solomon's temple. All the hype that had helped them through exile actually was not as good as it sounded. Reality did not match the hype.

Reality is like that in the aging process. When we are younger we are led to believe that all will be well when we get older. There will be time to do all those things we never had time to do— travel, get our spiritual lives in order, be with the family. Many times this is the way it is. However, sometimes the downside of the roller coaster hits—the death of a spouse, a serious illness that leaves us reeling and changes the rest of our lives. The hype about how great life is in the later years turns out not to be the reality.

When stark reality hits, the writer in Psalm 103 begins to focus on not forgetting all God's benefits. The people of God have to shift from focusing on the place, the temple, to focusing on the nature of the God they worship. Psalm 102 focuses on the psalmist himself and his finitude. Psalm 103 focuses on the nature of God. We are still on the mind of God, as we found from Psalm 8. Psalm 103 reaches for the broader picture. It does not deny finitude, but it is a reaffirmation of the providential care of God in the face of reality. The second temple was not like the first temple, and this was not only a disappointment, it was shattering to the people of God. They were back, they were facing change, and the bottom-line truth was that God had not deserted them.

WHAT DOES THE PSALM SAY?

Psalm 102

> Hear my prayer, O LORD;
>   let my cry come to you.
> Do not hide your face from me
>   in the day of my distress.
> Incline your ear to me;
>   answer me speedily in the day when I call.
> For my days pass away like smoke,
>   and my bones burn like a furnace.
> My heart is stricken and withered like grass;
>   I am too wasted to eat my bread.
> Because of my loud groaning
>   my bones cling to my skin.
> I am like an owl of the wilderness,
>   like a little owl of the waste places.
> I lie awake;
>   I am like a lonely bird on the housetop.
> All day long my enemies taunt me;
>   those who deride me use my name for a curse.
> For I eat ashes like bread,
>   and mingle tears with my drink,
> because of your indignation and anger;
>   for you have lifted me up and thrown me aside.
> My days are like an evening shadow;
>   I wither away like grass.
> But you, O LORD, are enthroned forever;
>   your name endures to all generations.

You will rise up and have compassion on Zion,
 for it is time to favor it;
 the appointed time has come.
For your servants hold its stones dear,
 and have pity on its dust.
The nations will fear the name of the LORD,
 and all the kings of the earth your glory.
For the LORD will build up Zion;
 he will appear in his glory.
He will regard the prayer of the destitute,
 and will not despise their prayer.
Let this be recorded for a generation to come,
 so that a people yet unborn may praise the LORD:
that he looked down from his holy height,
 from heaven the LORD looked at the earth,
to hear the groans of the prisoners,
 to set free those who were doomed to die;
so that the name of the LORD may be declared in Zion,
 and his praise in Jerusalem,
when peoples gather together,
 and kingdoms, to worship the LORD.
He has broken my strength in midcourse;
 he has shortened my days.
"O my God," I say, "do not take me away
 at the mid-point of my life,
you whose years endure
 throughout all generations."
Long ago you laid the foundation of the earth,
 and the heavens are the work of your hands.
They will perish, but you endure;
 they will all wear out like a garment.
You change them like clothing, and they pass away;
 but you are the same, and your years have no end.
The children of your servants shall live secure;
 their offspring shall be established in your presence.

Psalm 103

Bless the LORD, O my soul,
 and all that is within me,

bless his holy name.
Bless the LORD, O my soul,
    and do not forget all his benefits—
who forgives all your iniquity,
    who heals all your diseases,
who redeems your life from the Pit,
    who crowns you with steadfast love and mercy,
who satisfies you with good as long as you live
    so that your youth is renewed like the eagle's.
The LORD works vindication
    and justice for all who are oppressed.
He made known his ways to Moses,
    his acts to the people of Israel.
The LORD is merciful and gracious,
    slow to anger and abounding in steadfast love.
He will not always accuse,
    nor will he keep his anger forever.
He does not deal with us according to our sins,
    nor repay us according to our iniquities.
For as the heavens are high above the earth,
    so great is his steadfast love toward those who fear him;
as far as the east is from the west,
    so far he removes our transgressions from us.
As a father has compassion for his children,
    so the LORD has compassion for those who fear him.
For he knows how we were made;
    he remembers that we are dust.
As for mortals, their days are like grass;
    they flourish like a flower of the field;
for the wind passes over it, and it is gone,
    and its place knows it no more.
But the steadfast love of the LORD is from everlasting to
        everlasting
    on those who fear him,
    and his righteousness to children's children,
    to those who keep his covenant
    and remember to do his commandments.
The LORD has established his throne in the heavens,
    and his kingdom rules over all.

Bless the LORD, O you his angels,
    you mighty ones who do his bidding,
    obedient to his spoken word.
Bless the LORD, all his hosts,
    his ministers that do his will.
Bless the LORD, all his works,
    in all places of his dominion.
Bless the LORD, O my soul.

WHAT DO THESE PSALMS MEAN?

As you read through Psalm 102, you will notice that it has three very clear parts. *The Interpreter's Bible* lists these three sections as follows: (1) In verses 1–11, the psalmist provides a long list of personal difficulties and sufferings. Among those listed are illness, despair, loneliness, persecution, isolation, and the feeling that life no longer has meaning. (2) In verses 12–22, the psalmist turns from his inner turmoil to the external troubles around him, suggesting that perhaps his own personal troubles stem from his perception of the destruction of Jerusalem and his hope for its restoration. (3) In verses 23–28, once again, the psalmist speaks of personal troubles. Psalm 102 is filled with anguish, struggle, and complaint, both internal and external; these experiences are expressed in such clear images that almost anyone reading these words can identify directly.[2]

Psalm 103 is an exuberant, joyful hymn of gratitude to God for sins forgiven, for recovery from a serious illness, for new meaning in life and new energies to live life. It is a hymn of praise that begins and ends with gratitude to God, and it gives the rationale for the gratitude all through the hymn, naming God's blessings.

In Psalm 102, the writer deals with his own personal struggles, using a number of images to communicate the depth of his pain—a furnace, withered grass, a bird out of its usual habitat, eating food that tastes like ashes, and finding no meaning for life as the evening shadows appear. Then in Psalm 103, the psalmist begins and ends the hymn by blessing God for God's goodness and faithfulness. In between he recites the rationale for doing so, as in "The LORD works vindication and justice for all who are oppressed" (v. 6). Some of the benefits listed are forgiveness, healing, redemption, love and mercy, goodness and renewal. The obvious themes could be identified as lament in Psalm 102 and praise in Psalm 103. What other themes do you find in these two psalms, poignant with feeling and meaning?

Although Psalm 103 is more of a unit, or literary whole, than Psalm 102, they do share some common themes. Both speak of the transience of human beings, the permanent place of God as king, and the sure knowledge that God is compassionate toward those who are in difficulty. The main difference in the two psalms is that 102 is made up of personal lament, and 103 is composed of personal utterances of thanksgiving. What message do you think the psalmist had in mind for those who would sing or hear these hymns? You may want to explore further the images used in Psalm 102:3–11 for describing his situation, and then explore the list of reasons the psalmist gives in Psalm 103 for praising God. Is there a glimpse here into the answer to the question as to how the psalmist moves from despair to joy?

According to A. A. Anderson, Psalm 102 must have been written shortly after the end of the exile, since the pain and anguish are still quite evident.[3] Psalm 103 is clearly postexilic, reflecting the joy over how God has cared for all their needs during this time.

The words and phrases in these psalms are among the most heartrending and meaning-filled in the psalms. "My bones burn like a furnace" (102:3) could be a fever experienced by the author during a real illness, or it could also be a way of describing the horror of feeling that God has forgotten him. It may be both. That is, a real illness may be so bad the psalmist begins to feel that even God has forsaken him. The feelings of isolation from God seem to be a result of the affliction. Perhaps this is how life feels sometimes to persons with chronic arthritis or other painful maladies that can come in later life.

Another verse filled with feeling begins "My heart is stricken and withered like grass" (v. 4). This indicates that the troubles included more than simply an illness. Meaning has gone out of life, and the feeling of simply drying up and blowing away with the wind prevails. Cut off from life-sustaining strength, the heart withers and dies, just as grass. The pain continues in the second half of the verse: "I am too wasted to eat my bread." Loss of appetite when one is in great despair is a usual reaction. This loss of appetite could be caused by the illness, but the indication here is that because meaning has gone out of life, food is no longer a high priority.

One of the most poignant confessions in this psalm is "I am like a lonely bird on the housetop" (v. 7). The psalmist had spoken in verse 6 of being like a "little owl" in the waste places, perhaps meaning that he is out of his normal habitat. Both verses reflect the feeling that the psalmist is away from the familiar and alone in his misery, longing for familiar surroundings. In verse 10 the author is fully convinced that his troubles are a result of one source—divine punishment. God has taken away all help and healing, and this is why there is such despair. If God is punishing him, and is against him, what hope is there?

Finally, the focus is taken off the writer himself, and turns toward God: "But you, O LORD, are enthroned forever; your name endures to all generations" (v. 12). Even though the psalmist is suffering greatly, God is eternal, and those who love God can get through the difficulties by recognizing that God does not change. God is in charge, and this unchangeable God will bless them forever. The strength to endure must come from God, and if that directing and sustaining power is not in the picture, there is no hope. But with it all things are possible.

This thought leads to Psalm 103, where the writer reminds himself of all the benefits that God provides: "Do not forget all his benefits" (v. 2). The psalmist relates all the things that God has done for him personally. He is aware of God's forgiveness, God's healing, God's bringing hope to a life that had no hope, and God's bringing deep satisfaction and meaning once again to life. As the writer ponders his belief that what has happened to him is in some way a punishment, he writes, "He does not deal with us according to our sins, nor repay us according to our iniquities" (v. 10). This could be taken to mean that our sins are not punished, or that God does not pay us back for sinning by bringing punishment. However, it may refer more to God's desire to restore the sinner, not to destroy him or her. That is, God's punishment is tempered with God's mercy.

As the psalmist considers the nature of the God he worships, he shouts, "Bless the LORD, all his works, in all places of his do-

minion" (v. 22). Imagine what the world could be like if all people everywhere could sing this hymn in unison, act upon these
convictions, and live their lives blessing God in all places of
God's dominion!

This psalm raises an important question about older persons
who are experiencing some of the limitations brought on by the
aging process, such as diabetes, arthritis, and other chronic dis-
abilities. When a person can no longer physically get into the
church building, many times they lose that crucial link between
their own lives and the community of faith. This happens at a
time when the older person needs the church more than at any
other time in his or her life.

Since the fastest growing segment of the population is persons
eighty-five years of age and over, and since chronic and disabling diseases commonly come during those later years, this
has become a new "growing edge" of the church—to develop
ways to maintain the connection with homebound persons and
those in care facilities who can no longer get themselves to or
into the church facility. This ministry requires more than peri-
odic drop-in visits. It has to do with providing rituals to acknowledge and/or to celebrate the many transitions experienced
by those who are homebound or in nursing homes, to provide
opportunity to discuss spiritual issues, and to continue to build
relationships across the generational lines, even though they
cannot attend gatherings at the church.

WHAT DIFFERENCE DOES IT MAKE?

There are some theological and personal issues that might be
raised concerning these two psalms:

1. If God forgives all our iniquities, as in Psalm 103:3, why are
    we continually faced with and dealing with the results of
    our wrongdoing and wrong thinking? What difference does
    it make that God forgives our sins? We want to be set free
    from the effects of life's brokenness, to be healed of the in-
    juries life brings, to be rid of the guilt. Why doesn't God's
    forgiveness bring about this kind of freedom?

2. How are we to understand the psalmist when he says, "Do
    not forget all his benefits . . . who heals all your diseases"

(103:2–3)? The diseases of all persons are not healed, and many diseases cannot be healed. How is the reader to understand these verses?

3. If God "redeems your life from the Pit" (103:4a), why do we experience personal anguish, loneliness, and feelings of uselessness so much of the time?

4. If God "crowns you with steadfast love and mercy" (103:4b), why is there so much hate and lack of mercy shown, not only in the world, but also in the church?

5. If God "satisfies you with good as long as you live" (103:5), why do bad things happen to good people all the time?

6. How does the psalmist move from the Pit to the top of the mountain?

7. One of the underlying assumptions in these two psalms is that life is a gift to be celebrated, not a burden to be carried or endured. How does the psalmist create this kind of attitude toward life as reflected in Psalm 103 in the shadow of the anguish expressed in Psalm 102?

8. Why does God not hand out justice in an unjust world? How are we to understand injustice, oppression, and suffering? Where is God? Why doesn't God intervene?

9. What is the good news that these two psalms bring?

PUTTING IT ALL TOGETHER
AND BRINGING IT HOME

1. In Psalm 102:3–11, the psalmist lists a series of images to describe his situation: smoke, furnace, grass, a little owl, a lonely bird, eating ashes, evening shadows, and withering away. Identify the feeling that is expressed in each of these images. Which of these images most nearly fits your own thoughts and feelings at this time?

2. As indicated in Psalm 102:24, the psalmist seems to be middle-aged. When crises occur in our lives, whether in middle age or in later life, we begin to think of the inevitability and, perhaps, the imminence of death. When we first begin to think of the fact that someday we will die, it

comes as a shock. Why is this true, when death is as natural a part of life as birth, and as A Brief Statement of Faith (1994) of the Presbyterian Church (U.S.A.) suggests: "In life and in death we belong to God." If we really accepted death as a natural part of life, what difference would it make in how we live our lives each day?

3. As the psalmist ponders the nature of the God whom he worships, he thinks of the eternal sovereignty of God, the fact that God is actively engaged in the world (103:18–20), and he discovers that his thoughts have turned away from his own sufferings and have focused on God's faithfulness. He then finds the peace that he seeks. What clue does this give to you in dealing with your own suffering, despair, fears, and mortality? What difference could it make in your life if you changed your focus from your own struggles to the goodness of God?

HELPS FOR GROUP STUDY

A. Begin the session by reading Psalms 102 and 103 from the NRSV. This can be done by having one person read one psalm and another person read the second psalm, or if all participants have the same translation they could read it antiphonally. Then read the psalms again, one verse at a time from various translations, if possible, and compare the different translations. Are there significant differences? If so, discuss the different meanings that the different translations give to the verses.

B. Review the list of struggles found in Psalm 102:3–11 and discuss what might have been going on in the life of the author to cause him to be in such anguish. What might have been the occasion for his writing it?

C. Identify the key words, images, or phrases that give a hint as to the message of the psalmist for his readers. Why are these important? What is the hint they give about the message?

D. Explore with the group what they believe the psalmist is saying to the people of his day.

ʼE. Discuss with the group the theological and personal issues raised by the psalms as listed under "What Difference Does It Make?" and others that the group may raise.

F. What is the message of these two psalms to today's world, and to the participants in the study group?

G. Discuss how a person in today's world can live on the roller coaster of life and still live a life of gratitude to God. How can such a person move from the depths to the heights as did the psalmist?

H. As a final exercise, it might be interesting to match up the blessings listed in Psalm 103 with the images of despair listed in the first part of Psalm 102.

I. Ask the participants to write a psalm of pure praise for all the blessings of being an older person!

Notes

1. James L. Mays, *Psalms,* Interpretation: A Bible Commentary for Teaching and Preaching (Louisville, Ky.: John Knox Press, 1994), 324.

2. *The Interpreter's Bible,* vol. 4 (Nashville: Abingdon Press, 1955), 539.

3. A. A. Anderson, *Psalms,* The New Century Bible Commentary, vol. 2 (Grand Rapids: Wm. B. Eerdmans Publishing Co., and London: Marshall, Morgan & Scott Publishing, 1972), 704.

Chapter 5

Psalms 42 and 43
BEING IN A PLACE WHERE
I DON'T WANT TO BE

*There is nothing that the Christian interpreter has to
do to place the Psalms in the hands of his or her
congregation. That congregation has carried this song
book under its arm throughout all the centuries of
worship. . . . The Psalms have not been simply read
as Scripture from the past but have been sung as
words in and for the present.*
—Patrick D. Miller Jr.

INTRODUCTION

One afternoon while visiting in the intermediate care unit of
the retirement community where I was chaplain, I was asked by
the nurse to seek out and talk with Mrs. B. The nurse said Mrs.
B. fell frequently in her room, and there did not seem to be a reason for it. I found Mrs. B. sitting by herself on the terrace, looking out at the beautiful wooded area before her. I introduced
myself, sat down beside her, and asked her about her family. She
had a daughter who lived in California who came about every
other year for a weeklong visit. I asked about her church mem-
bership and learned that she had been a very loyal, active member of one of the largest churches in the city. She had been
president of the women's organization of the church, taught
Sunday school for twenty-five years, and was at the church every
time the doors opened. I asked her if members of the church visited. Her reply shocked me. She said that the new pastor came
to visit about six months ago but that he seemed very ill at ease
and uncomfortable, did not stay very long, and had not been
back to see her.

I then said to her, "The nurse told me that you fall frequently in your room. Do you get up too quickly and become dizzy and fall, or do you stumble on the carpet? Do we need to get you some other kind of shoes to wear?" Mrs. B. looked down for a long time. When she finally raised her head she looked embarrassed and hesitant. Then she said, "I do that deliberately, because when I fall on the floor and call out, someone comes and puts their arms around me and helps me to get up." She touched the skin on the back of her hand, and said, "My skin gets so hungry!" That prompted a "hug Mrs. B." campaign so that each time a staff person passed her, it was "hug time."

I called the church and told them this story, and the church began regular weekly visits with Mrs. B. Within a few weeks Mrs. B. was a completely changed person. She became outgoing and friendly, and she visited others on her floor, helping to take care of them. She felt like a whole person again. Here was a well-educated woman from upper-middle-class Atlanta society, who had spent her life working in the church and who was reduced to falling on the floor and calling for help—so great was her need to be touched, hugged, recognized as a person, and to feel loved.

We human beings, especially in the later years of life, experience times when our sense of God's presence fades or vanishes. This can be brought on by the death of someone close, a broken relationship, a serious illness, or some other transition that brings trauma into our lives. It can also come about by just drifting along with the day-to-day routines without paying attention to the spiritual side of life, or by not having daily interchange with other human beings. As a result, we feel abandoned, we live in darkness and with great anxiety. That is what the writer of Psalms 42 and 43 was experiencing when he wrote so graphically concerning his feelings.

Psalms 42 and 43 are among the most touching of all the psalms. The thoughts expressed, the words used, the conditions under which they seem to have been written, have a familiar ring to many older adults. They seem to have been written by one who has been uprooted from home and all that is familiar. Because of this, the psalmist expresses a sense of desolation when he remembers his participation in the services in his home community a long time ago: "These things I remember, as I pour out my soul: how I went with the throng, and led them in procession" (42:4). As if his homesickness and the pain of remembering were not enough, he also seems to have some physical illness and may have been near death, as reflected in verse 7: "Deep calls to deep at the thunder of your cataracts." Then, beyond this, he experiences criticism from those around him. He feels that he has been abandoned by society, by friends, and even by God. However, through what W. O. E. Oesterley calls a process of "self-communing,"[1] the psalmist gains some measure of comfort and strength in his grief through his remembering times past when he went with the community of worshipers to his own familiar place of worship.

What makes this psalm so appealing to older adults? What is the yearning expressed in the psalm all about? Is remembering the past helpful in facing the present and the future? Doesn't remembering make the pain and the grief worse? How can remembering be helpful? With these questions in mind, read and ponder the psalm.

WHAT DOES THE PSALM SAY?

Psalm 42

> As a deer longs for flowing streams,
>   so my soul longs for you, O God.
> My soul thirsts for God,
>   for the living God.
> When shall I come and behold
>   the face of God?
> My tears have been my food
>   day and night,
> while people say to me continually,
>   "Where is your God?"
> These things I remember,
>   as I pour out my soul:
> how I went with the throng,
>   and led them in procession to the house of God,
> with glad shouts and songs of thanksgiving,
>   a multitude keeping festival.

Why are you cast down, O my soul,
    and why are you disquieted within me?
Hope in God; for I shall again praise him,
    my help and my God.
My soul is cast down within me;
    therefore I remember you
from the land of Jordan and of Hermon,
    from Mount Mizar.
Deep calls to deep
    at the thunder of your cataracts;
all your waves and your billows
    have gone over me.
By day the LORD commands his steadfast love,
    and at night his song is with me,
    a prayer to the God of my life.
I say to God, my rock,
    "Why have you forgotten me?
Why must I walk about mournfully
    because the enemy oppresses me?"
As with a deadly wound in my body,
    my adversaries taunt me,
while they say to me continually,
    "Where is your God?"
Why are you cast down, O my soul,
    and why are you disquieted within me?
Hope in God; for I shall again praise him,
    my help and my God.

Psalm 43

Vindicate me, O God, and defend my cause
    against an ungodly people;
from those who are deceitful and unjust
    deliver me!
For you are the God in whom I take refuge;
    why have you cast me off?
Why must I walk about mournfully
    because of the oppression of the enemy?
O send out your light and your truth;
    let them lead me;

let them bring me to your holy hill
   and to your dwelling.
Then I will go to the altar of God,
   to God my exceeding joy;
and I will praise you with the harp,
   O God, my God.
Why are you cast down, O my soul,
   and why are you disquieted within me?
Hope in God; for I shall again praise him,
   my help and my God.

Psalms 42 and 43 are about discovering that we have limitations, that as we get older we experience some changes in our bodies. I realized this fact in a painful and realistic manner during a vacation with a friend in the Florida Keys. We drove to Key West and rented bicycles in order to really see the island. After taking a sunset cruise in a glass-bottomed boat, and viewing the beauty of the fish life under the clear waters around the island, we arrived back to our bicycles after dark. We found ourselves weaving in and out of traffic (downtown we could not ride on the sidewalks), and with no lights on the bicycles, it was rather treacherous. However, we soon reached the highway beside the water, and we were allowed to use the wide, though unlighted, sidewalks. My friend, younger than I, soon was far ahead of me. I was peddling as fast as I dared under the circumstances. I was breathing hard, my knees hurt something awful, my back ached, and at times I thought I would not make it back to the motel. And I was not sure my knees and leg muscles would manage even walking at that point! As I was struggling along in the dark I thought back ten years, and how I would have been racing anyone else I was riding with. I learned through this experience that I cannot do what I did ten years ago.

My body is not what it was, and even though I walk a mile or so every day, I have to accept the fact that change is taking place in my body. This was driven home when I did finally arrive at the motel, and was in excruciating pain for about an hour with leg cramps. That was a hard fact to accept, since I like to think of myself as about fifteen years younger than I actually am! Physical limitations, spiritual yearnings, depression, and feelings of abandonment, all of which can be brought on by the aging process, mean that we find ourselves in a state in which we don't want to be. Feelings of uselessness and isolation abound, and it is not unusual for depression to become a part of everyday life. We need affirmation that life has been worthwhile, and that we still have a role in life and a contribution to make. How did the psalmist deal with these feelings? A detailed look at the psalms may be helpful.

The background of Psalms 42 and 43 is uncertain. Some scholars think that these psalms originated in the Northern Kingdom and reflect the period just before, or at the time of, the fall of Samaria in 721 B.C.E. William Holladay says "there are two interlocking kinds of evidence. The first is the references to geographical features or tribes of the north such as references to 'the Jordan,' and 'Mount Hermon' which suggests a locale at the headwaters of the River Jordan in Upper Galilee. The second kind of evidence is language usage in the Hebrew text that exhibits northern dialect."[2] If this is the case, these writings could have been some of the material that undoubtedly made its way from the north to the south after the fall of the Northern Kingdom.

If this is true, we must be careful how we read the historical context of Psalm 42:4: "These things I remember, as I pour out my soul: how I went with the throng, and led them in procession to the house of God." At first these verses might seem to reflect the cult as it operated around the temple of Jerusalem, but this would be inconsistent with the date of 721 B.C.E. While undoubtedly the cult flourished in Jerusalem, cultic worship at that time had not been centralized. This verse may represent ceremonies that occurred in local shrines such as Dan, Bethel, and Shechem. Therefore, we cannot assume that the "house of God" refers to the temple in Jerusalem. This makes little difference in our study of the verse, but this is just to present the possible historical context of the psalms.

It is possible that the opening verse of Psalm 42 ("As a deer longs for flowing streams, so my soul longs for you, O God") is a reference to a catastrophe, such as the fall of Samaria to the Assyrians. This psalm could reflect that the writer had been deported and is remembering that he used to go to the local shrines and places of worship, but can no longer.

Whatever the case, the writer is reflecting on the fact that he can no longer be part of the worshiping community as a regular participant, and that he is physically separated from it. This may be captivity. It may be illness or infirmity. It is not possible to know for sure. What we are aware of is the anguish that this physical and spiritual separation causes the psalmist. He thinks back on what his worship life used to be like.

The psalmist's constant hope is that even though he finds himself in an isolated and alienated situation he will find a way to reconnect. Verse 7 may indicate that the pull of the community's faith is still with him. The "deep calls to deep" could be a reference to what it is like to be a part of the community, but unable to actively take part in it, bringing forth a call from the deep places of soul to connect up again.

Verse 10 is significant. The foes who ask, "Where is your God?" may be real live human beings, or it could be that the psalmist is simply not taking steps to maintain the connections between those in "exile" and those within the faith community. For instance, if you are a homebound person or live in a care facility and can no longer go to worship services in the church that you have loved and served all of your life, and no one from the church comes to visit, this can feel like a "taunt" by your "foes."

The psalmist is experiencing a narrowing of community encounter. This can sometimes be a part of the aging process—widowhood, physical infirmity, sight or hearing impairment, loss of full mobility—all of which can bring about a narrowing of the world for that person. If all a person can do is sit in a chair or lie in bed all day, looking out at the world from inside, the world can become very small and very narrow, and one can become concerned only with the very basic routines of life and not stimulated to widen the horizons.

Loss of hearing is one of the most common and most frustrating of the "foes." Hearing loss brings about a terrible narrowing of one's world. It is a kind of captivity, a foreign land, and a person can become almost paranoid because of it. When people experience loss of hearing it is very difficult for them to be in community with others. They like to be in community, but their physical disadvantage imprisons them because they have lost the discernment that comes with hearing. People who are hearers find it very difficult because, on the surface, the person with hearing impairment does not look any different from anyone else. Responses of anger from members of the community because of the impairment only cause a further breaking of the connection with the community of faith.

People who are imprisoned like this sometimes tend to look as though they are miles away in another place. Because their world is so narrow they fall back on what Oesterley calls, "self-communing,"[3] and they deal with their interior world, concentrating on their own situation and the past. This can be a real strength if they can find God in the midst of it. But they need help to do this. That world can be very negative, depending upon their experiences. The question is: How do we help people to maintain those connections with God, with other people, and with their true self, despite their physical limitations?

The major themes in the psalm seem to be loneliness and a yearning for the familiar (vv. 1–2), the pain and the blessing of remembering (v. 4), the value of self-communing (vv. 5, 11), and the power of mockery when one is depressed (vv. 3, 10).

In Psalm 43:1–5 the writer begins with a prayer. The struggle that had gone on within the psalmist is now quieted. He begins to long for God for God's own sake, for the sake of communion with God, not so much for what God can give him. When he comes to this point he rebukes himself once again for his despair and doubt. He discovers that life is empty and meaningless without an awareness of the presence of God in the community of faith; that human beings can move from utter despair to firm hope, knowing that the times of despair will come again, as will the times of hope.

Another important message in Psalm 42 is what Oesterley calls "the act of religious self-communing," as mentioned earlier. The theme seems significant since the psalmist refers over and over again to his soul, as if it were a separate and distinct entity from himself: "Why are you cast down, O my soul" (42:5), and in the same breath he identifies with it: "as I pour out my soul" (42:4). He rebukes his soul for its despair, and in the next breath he immediately proclaims his faith in God. The psalmist is in the midst of a deep personal struggle, of trying to understand his despair, and at the same time to hang on to and to bring his faith in God to bear upon his situation.

WHAT DOES THE PSALM MEAN?

It will be helpful to look at some key words and phrases to seek the message of this psalm.

1. "Flowing streams" (42:1) could refer to the perennial streams that flow and never dry up even during the dry season. A. A. Anderson has drawn a correlation between "flowing streams" and "living waters," suggesting that the psalmist may be saying that Yahweh is "the fountain of living waters." This can also be seen in Jeremiah 17:13: "All who forsake you shall be put to shame; those who turn away from you shall be recorded in the underworld, for they have forsaken the fountain of living water, the LORD."[4] The idea is that those living waters will never dry up. They will always be available to bring new life.

2. "So my soul longs for you, O God" (42:1) suggests that just as a long dry spell drives animals in search of life-sustaining water, so the troubles of the psalmist increase his yearning for life-sustaining closeness with God. The psalmist seems to be saying that this is the way it is with the heart's longing for God. In Kenya, a tourist can go to a hotel outside Nairobi where there is a waterhole for the animals that roam the hills. The animals come all through the night, and at any time the tourist can go out onto a balcony and see rhinos, elephants, giraffes, and many other wild animals native to that area. Some of those animals travel long distances in order to receive the life-sustaining water that is available at the waterhole.

3. "Where is your God?" (42:3) may be a sarcastic question from fellow human beings. This phrase is found frequently in the Psalms, such as 79:10 and 115:2. The implication is that either God is powerless to do anything about the sufferings of the psalmist, or God does not care about him. This question has puzzled scholars for centuries, and no one has found clear answers as to why God doesn't intervene and "fix things." After all, isn't God all-powerful, and doesn't God love creation inclusively?

4. "These things I remember . . . " (42:4) could indicate that the psalmist finds some comfort in a deliberate recalling of certain cherished things in his past, especially those connected with activities in the house of God when he was much younger. Robert Davidson says of this verse, "Here is a person who once

joyfully participated with his fellow worshipers in one of the great religious festivals centering on the temple. What that meant to him is indelibly imprinted on his memory. It is there, part of his life, to be placed over against the bleakness of his present plight."[5]

5. "My soul is cast down within me; therefore I remember you" (42:6) seems to suggest that because the psalmist is in despair he remembers his relationship with God, and he yearns for it in order to give vent to all his pent-up frustrations, anger, and longings as he "pours out" his soul. "The anguish of God's absence is answered by remembrance. . . . [T]he speaker remembers having praised God joyfully in the midst of the worshiping congregation, and contrasts his feelings of isolation and alienation with his memories of God's closeness during corporate worship."[6]

6. "Deep calls to deep" (42:7) is a very difficult phrase to interpret. The traditional view is that it refers to some illness of the psalmist. However, it could refer to the depths of despair calling one to deeper despair. As mentioned before, it could refer to the yearning of the heart to maintain the connection with the community of faith. A very positive view of the passage could mean that the deepest within the heart of human beings calls out to the deepest within the heart of God. The reverse is also true: the deepest within the heart of God calls out to the deepest within the heart of humans. The International Critical Commentary has an interesting view. It suggests that the phrase personifies the waters (as in "calling aloud in their roaring descent"), that the psalmist feels overwhelmed, submerged, and drowning in his troubles.[7] Davidson indicates that the word "deep" has "echoes of the forces of chaos which threaten orderly life, and the whole verse may be no more than a highly poetic way of saying that the psalmist now feels overwhelmed by the chaotic forces of despair threatening to destroy him."[8]

7. "Hope in God" (42:5, 11) turns what had been a yearning remembrance into a joyful hope. The struggle has quieted and the psalmist has accepted life as it is, hoping that the God who has been present in the past will be present into the future.

WHAT DIFFERENCE DOES IT MAKE?

Some theological issues that emerge from Psalms 42 and 43 are:

1. What is the difference between self-communing or communion with God? and prayer? A person in difficulty can seek help from many places, but ultimately the person must face himself or herself and resolve the issue, or decide to accept it and move on. The psalmist does this in a graphic manner by entering into dialogue with the self or the soul. How is this different from prayer to God?

2. What are the theological implications of the psalmist's claim that God had forgotten him? What does this say about the psalmist's view of God?

3. What does the psalm teach about the nature of God? About human beings?

4. How does the psalmist move from the despair in Psalm 42:1–3 to the ecstatic praise of God in Psalm 43:3–4?

Some personal issues are identified in this psalm that are quite familiar to all humans, and especially to some older persons. Go back through the psalm and identify the feelings that are presented, such as yearning, grief over loss, self-rebuke, anger, and anxiety. Questions to ponder include:

1. How does the psalmist deal with his despair?

2. How does the psalmist deal with criticism and self-doubt?

3. How is remembering helpful to the psalmist in dealing with despair?

4. How is it helpful for a person to "pour out" the soul? Or, is it helpful?

PUTTING IT ALL TOGETHER
AND BRINGING IT HOME

1. Which of the issues or themes in Psalms 42 and 43 most nearly touch your own struggles?

2. What is the central message of these psalms for you in your present circumstances? With which verses do you most easily identify? What are these verses saying to you at this time in your life?

3. Ponder the question: If God is really present in my life, why do I sometimes have, like the psalmist, a deep yearning inside me, and feel as though I am living in spiritual darkness?

HELPS FOR GROUP LEADERS

A. Read the psalm one verse at a time in the group with group members participating as they wish. Notice particularly the differences in the various translations.

B. Discuss what seem to be significant differences in the various translations.

C. What seems to have been going on in the life of the psalmist when he wrote these psalms?

D. Discuss key words, images, or phrases in these psalms that provide clues to clarify feelings, such as the image of the thirsty animal longing for a cool stream, the waves of water engulfing the psalmist, and words or phrases such as "remember," "hope," "cast down," "my rock," and "send out your light and your truth; let them lead me."

E. Ask the participants to explore what they believe the message of the psalm is for today.

F. In what way is the message for older adults today different from the message to the psalmist's first readers? In what way is it similar?

G. Ask the participants to think back to their young adulthood and share the most significant experience they had as a young adult in relationship with God. Was this at a crisis time in their life? How does looking back on the experience years later help in interpreting how God worked in the situation?

H. Ask the participants to think of a time when they felt that God had abandoned them. What did that feel like? Ask how they worked through that kind of despair.

I. Ask the participants to think of a time when they felt most intensely the presence of God.

J. Suggest to the participants that they might enjoy individually writing their own psalm concerning the feelings talked about in the study of the many moods in Psalms 42 and 43.

K.   Read Psalm 23 and discuss how the mood of Psalm 23 is different from that found in Psalms 42 and 43.

Notes

1. W. O. E. Oesterley, *The Psalms* (London: SPCK, 1959), 240.

2. William L. Holladay, *The Psalms through Three Thousand Years* (Minneapolis: Fortress Press, 1993), 27.

3. Oesterley, *Psalms,* 240.

4. A. A. Anderson, *Psalms,* The New Century Bible Commentary, vol. I (Grand Rapids: Wm. B. Eerdmans Publishing Co. and London: Marshall, Morgan & Scott Publishing, 1972), 329.

5. Robert Davidson, *The Vitality of Worship: A Commentary on the Book of Psalms* (Grand Rapids: Wm. B. Eerdmans Publishing Co., 1998), 142–43.

6. Charles A. Briggs and Emilie Grace Briggs, *The Book of Psalms,* International Critical Commentary (Edinburgh: T. & T. Clark, 1976), 370.

7. Ibid.

8. Davidson, *Vitality of Worship,* 143.

Chapter 6

Psalm 71
WHAT SHALL I DO WITH THE REST OF MY LIFE?

*Hence it is that the Psalter is the book of all saints;
and everyone, in whatever situation he may be, finds
in that situation Psalms and words that fit his case,
so that he could not put it better himself, or find or
wish for anything better.*

—Martin Luther

INTRODUCTION

Society tells people what they must do when they retire: Sit in a rocking chair, travel, watch TV, and certainly just get out of the way and don't interfere. Many retired persons buy into society's stereotype of older persons and what they are to do. As a result, older adults are marginalized by society, put on the shelf as it were, and denied the privilege of sharing the wisdom of their years. All of us are the losers when this happens.

Many retired persons are much busier in retirement than they ever were during their work life. They continue the ministry of the church, mentor in schools, write books, counsel younger people, and give of themselves and their talents to the limit of their physical abilities. Some would like to be involved in this way, but have not been able to find just the right role for themselves. Psalm 71 may bring hope into their lives.

There are at least two kinds of older people in the church—those who cannot give up their position, and those who, when they retire from their work life and responsibility, also retire from their church life and responsibility. In the case of the first ones mentioned, although their wisdom is still needed (but perhaps not in an official setting) they cannot turn loose the position of control they have held for many years. Even though they are not on the board or committee anymore, they maintain their traditions and authority, and find it very difficult to turn "their" responsibility over to another person. Many times when they do turn over their responsibility to someone else, they retreat from any responsibility at all, and sometimes drop out of the church altogether. There are "mine fields" all over the church—in the kitchen, in the choir, on the grounds, at the organ, and other places—where older persons say, "I have always done this; what are you doing here?" Much of this has to do with control and identity. If they choose to drop out, taking their faith journey with them, this is a loss to all concerned.

In the case of the second category, they say, "I've been there, done that," and they sit back and begin to live on the periphery of the church. Some even choose not to be connected to the church at all. As with families, there is a system in every church. We have a need to know what our place is in the system, and one of the hard things about being an older adult is that we are still in the system, but are faced with a status change. In many respects, it has to do with a sense of belonging. You belong because you have a place in the system. Many of us don't know how to handle a status change, and the church as a whole also has difficulty with it. Churches are like families, and when change comes it is sometimes difficult to work out where one's place is.

Part of the difficulty is that *we* change, physically and otherwise, in the aging process. We are not the way we used to be. We know without a doubt that we cannot do what we used to do, although most of the time we see ourselves as we were at an earlier time and feel that we can do the same things we did then. Former President Jimmy Carter quotes his friend and "mountain philosopher" Jimmy Townsend: "Anybody who can still do at sixty what he was doing at twenty wasn't doing much at twenty."[1] One of the responsibilities of the church is to help older persons to accept who they are currently, to get in touch with their true selves now, not how they were years ago. Psalm 90:12 says it well: "Teach us to number our days aright, that we may gain a heart of wisdom" (NIV).

Psalm 71 has been called the "Older Adult's Psalm." It is classified as a psalm of lament, a cry for help, but that is not all it is. It is also a hymn of joy and praise. *The Interpreter's Bible* surmises that the writer had to make it clear that he is an older adult and not a youth, that since the psalm in some places is so exuberant one could mistake the psalmist for a much younger person.[2] The writer is especially exuberant when he expresses his gratitude to God for God's faithfulness through the years, and for this he makes a promise: "Even to old age and gray hairs, O God, do not forsake me, until I proclaim your might to all the generations to come" (71:18). In so doing, the psalmist outlines the proper and true role, or calling, for older persons—to tell the stories of God's deeds of mercy to all the generations to come.

WHAT DOES THE PSALM SAY?

Psalm 71

> In you, O LORD, I take refuge;
>> let me never be put to shame.
> In your righteousness deliver me and rescue me;
>> incline your ear to me and save me.
> Be to me a rock of refuge,
>> a strong fortress, to save me,
>> for you are my rock and my fortress.
> Rescue me, O my God, from the hand of the wicked,
>> from the grasp of the unjust and cruel.
> For you, O Lord, are my hope,
>> my trust, O LORD, from my youth.
> Upon you I have leaned from my birth;
>> it was you who took me from my mother's womb.
> My praise is continually of you.
> I have been like a portent to many,
>> but you are my strong refuge.
> My mouth is filled with your praise,
>> and with your glory all day long.
> Do not cast me off in the time of old age;
>> do not forsake me when my strength is spent.
> For my enemies speak concerning me,
>> and those who watch for my life consult together.

They say, "Pursue and seize that person
    whom God has forsaken,
    for there is no one to deliver."
O God, do not be far from me,
    O my God, make haste to help me!
Let my accusers be put to shame and consumed;
    let those who seek to hurt me
    be covered with scorn and disgrace.
But I will hope continually,
    and will praise you yet more and more.
My mouth will tell of your righteous acts,
    of your deeds of salvation all day long,
    though their number is past my knowledge.
I will come praising the mighty deeds of the Lord GOD,
    I will praise your righteousness, yours alone.
O God, from my youth you have taught me,
    and I still proclaim your wondrous deeds.
So even to old age and gray hairs,
    O God, do not forsake me,
until I proclaim your might
    to all the generations to come.
Your power and your righteousness, O God,
    reach the high heavens.
You who have done great things,
    O God, who is like you?
You who have made me see many troubles and calamities
    will revive me again;
from the depths of the earth
    you will bring me up again.
You will increase my honor,
    and comfort me once again.
I will also praise you with the harp
    for your faithfulness, O my God;
I will sing praises to you with the lyre,
    O Holy One of Israel.
My lips will shout for joy
    when I sing praises to you;
    my soul also, which you have rescued.
All day long my tongue will talk of your righteous help,

for those who tried to do me harm
have been put to shame, and disgraced.

WHAT DOES THE PSALM MEAN?

In Psalm 71, the writer refers to the past, the present, and the future somewhat like the three movements of a symphony. In a symphony, in the first movement, there is the introductory theme that is fixed firmly in the listener's mind before moving on. The theme in this psalm shows the psalmist facing the realities of life. It is filled with anxiety, struggle, and hurt. This is not a dream world we live in, but life is difficult and filled with anguish, as in, "Rescue me, O my God, from the hand of the wicked" (v. 4).

In the second movement of most symphonies, there is usually an exploration of the theme and its various aspects, a fleshing out of the theme in all of its highest and lowest emotions. This also happens in the psalm. The writer remembers the hurts and the taunting from enemies, and expresses the depths of despair, but during that exploration, he discovers that, even during the hurtful times, he finds comfort and hope: "I will hope continually, and will praise you yet more and more" (v. 14). Even in his old age, he is still being taught, still learning: "O God, from my youth you have taught me" (v. 17).

In the third movement of many symphonies, there is usually an effort to bring some resolution or closure to the heights and depths of emotion that have emerged during the first and second movements. The aspects of the theme are still remembered, and some resolution or completion is attempted. Usually, the resolution is not complete, but the music finishes with a grand finale that brings an exciting conclusion to the symphony. In Psalm 71, the mood changes dramatically in the final verses, as the psalmist looks toward spending the rest of his days singing praises to God for God's faithfulness and goodness to him throughout his life: "Even to old age and gray hairs, O God, do not forsake me, until I proclaim your might to all the generations to come. Your power and your righteousness, O God, reach the high heavens" (v. 18).

The image that the psalmist provides for the role of the older persons in society is quite different from contemporary society's stereotype of the retired person The psalmist, with determined faith and hope, writes that he will sing and tell about God's mercy to the end of his days, for he has a lifelong story to share of the faithfulness of a great God. What a beautiful final movement in life's symphony! As one commentary states it: "He has lived a full life; he has reflected on its triumphs and its disasters, and he has pronounced it good. God, the Holy One of Israel, be praised!"[3] Oesterley puts it this way: "He can look back upon his past life in the happy conviction that he has done his duty to God; and that, in spite of troubles, God has been with him and upheld him."[4]

Psalm 31, especially verses 1–3, is quite similar to Psalm 71. Some scholars believe that the writer of Psalm 71 is quoting from Psalm 31, but others think the similarities may come from the writer's knowledge of language that was common to this type of writing at that time. Most scholars place the psalm during the postexilic period because the writer seems to be knowledgeable about written material in the psalms that is also of that time. If this dating is correct, it means that the times through which the psalmist lived were not particularly peaceful times. It is interesting that the author does not mention his own children or grandchildren, usually seen to be among the greatest benefits of becoming older. Exiles, while either staying in a foreign land or returning to a homeland that had been destroyed, did not live in particularly tranquil or happy times, and many times discovered that none of their kin survived.[5]

A look at some words and phrases might be helpful in discerning what the psalm is saying:

1. "Be to me a rock of refuge, a strong fortress, to save me, for you are my rock and my fortress" (v. 3). The psalmist seems to have reached the end of his rope, and in this hour of great despair he turns to God, who has never failed to help him through times of crisis in the past, and whose praises he has never stopped singing. "This psalmist unashamedly draws on the rich heritage of faith of his people and finds in it a 'safe haven' in the face of hostility which might otherwise have destroyed him."[6]

2. "Let my accusers be put to shame and consumed; let those who seek to hurt me be covered with scorn and disgrace" (v. 13).

The psalmist makes a second appeal here, asking that his accusers be disgraced publicly. In the ancient Near East public disgrace was the most difficult to bear, worse than death (see Job
29:7–10). It is not clear exactly what the crisis was in the life of
the psalmist. However, there seem to be people who want to take
advantage of his troubles and interpret the trouble as a sign of
God's judgment. How can you put verse 13 together with the
New Testament idea found in Matthew 5:43–45: "You have
heard that it was said, 'You shall love your neighbor and hate
your enemy.' But I say to you, Love your enemies and pray for
those who persecute you, so that you may be children of your
Father in heaven"?

3. "Rescue me, O my God. . . . For you, O Lord, are my hope,
my trust" (vv. 4–5), is a prayer for help and deliverance from a
series of difficulties. The psalm focuses on assertions of trust to
the extent that trust in God far outweighs the psalmist's concern
with his troubles. How do you think the psalmist gets to the
place where he prays as much or more about his trust and confidence in God as he does in laying out his troubles?

4. "I have been like a portent to many" (v. 7). There are di-
verse opinions among scholars as to the meaning of *portent.*
Oesterley translates it "a wonderment to many," and suggests
that it has to do with "a contemptible spectacle causing aston-
ishment," probably referring to some malady from which the
psalmist was suffering.[7] Others translate it a "solemn warning,"[8]
or "a terrible example of divine vengeance."[9] The fact is the true
meaning is not clear. If we follow Oesterley it could be a positive
meaning; if we follow the others it could be a negative meaning.
The Oxford Dictionary of Current English defines *portent* as "an
omen, a significant sign of something to come, or a prodigy (an
exceptionally gifted child), a marvelous thing."[10] If we accept
this definition, where does it lead in understanding this psalm?

5. "Do not cast me off in the time of old age; do not forsake
me when my strength is spent" (v. 9). A paradox is evident here.
The psalmist wrote in verse 5 that he has trusted in God and
found his hope in God from his youth. Yet, four verses later, he
is pleading with God not to cast him off in his old age. Perhaps
he is fearful that (as in modern U.S. society) when he becomes
older, he will no longer be seen to have value to society.

Our society, including the church, focuses on youth and youthfulness almost to the point of worship. Think about it. We older people want to look and act youthful for as long as possible. We spend millions of dollars each year on cosmetics that are designed to cover up the signs of aging, or on cosmetic surgery to achieve the same goal. Value in our society is based on productivity. So when a person is no longer productive, as society interprets productivity, the person is seen to be of no value anymore. Of course, we don't want to tell or look our age! Just look at the birthday cards that make fun of the limitations brought on by the aging process, such as loss of hearing, sight, and memory, slowness of movement, and the decline in interest in sex, together with black balloons and crepe paper announcing that age forty is "over the hill." It is no wonder that we don't like to tell our age, and try to cover up and deny our aging process. There are a few birthday cards that give a positive view of aging. One that I saw recently said, "Youth is a gift; age is an art!" But, on the whole, to be old in America is to be unacceptable, and so we focus on acting and looking as young as we can for as long as we can. If this is what the psalmist surmises, it is no wonder that he feels that God seems to be far away. However, Anderson points out the comforting thought that the God of the psalmist's youth is still the God of his old age, as in Isaiah 46:4: "Even to your old age I am he, even when you turn gray I will carry you. I have made, and I will bear; I will carry and will save."[11] Therefore, an unchangeable God could not be a different God to youth and older persons, but the same God who promises never to forsake regardless of the age or the ability to produce.

6. "So even to old age and gray hairs, O God, do not forsake me, until I proclaim your might to all the generations to come" (v. 18). Although the psalmist calls out to God for deliverance, as we have seen, the dominant theme is that of the psalmist affirming his faith in God, and expressing gratitude to God for God's care throughout his life, for God's faithfulness through many struggles, and for God's mercy. So we can say of the psalmist that he has written his own affirmation of faith in this psalm. Then, as a crowning effort of praise, the psalmist promises to tell stories of God's might and power and righteousness to all generations to come. *The New Interpreter's Bible* puts it this way:

"Although having grown old, the psalmist expects new things, indeed, the psalmist is intent on proclaiming God's deeds to generations to come. . . . All who belong to God are called to praise God continually (v. 6) in joyful gratitude for God's faithfulness and righteousness (vv. 22–24), to witness to all the generations to come (v. 18) that ultimately nothing 'will be able to separate us from the love of God'" (Romans 8:39, NRSV).[12]

One of the difficulties in sharing the stories of God's might to other generations is the reluctance of other generations, both above and below in age, to listen and hear. In churches, as well as in society generally, we have been so successful in separating the ages in Sunday schools, church activities, projects, and daily routines that we hardly know how to talk with each other across generational lines. In previous generations there was the family farm or the family business, where all generations worked together as a team. Schools were the center of community activities, and whole families were involved in social events and projects. And in churches, even if classes were divided by age, they usually began and ended with an assembly where all generations were together. Now the parents go to work in some other location away from home, the children go to school in another community away from home, and in church the ages are divided into classes, and the children are usually sent out of the worship service after the children's sermon to another place for other kinds of activities.

One of the challenges for the church is to develop ways to bring the generations together so that sharing can take place across generational lines. The young people need the wisdom of the older people who have lived long and know where the pitfalls are, and what works and what fails. The older people need the younger people to teach them how to live in a society that changes by quantum leaps daily, and to teach them the new technologies that are required for living in the present world. These have to be intentional efforts, because in present society intergenerational interchange does not happen automatically.

Another concern raised by verse 18 has to do with the giving and receiving of advice across generational lines. Listening and hearing do not happen automatically between generations, and so a high level of intentionality is needed so that the sharing will work. Grace given has to be matched by grace received. That is, the graciousness with which the sharing of a story is received also exhibits a faith story for the next generation. A person can proclaim God's gracious deeds by graciously receiving them.

In the movie *Driving Miss Daisy* (starring Jessica Tandy, Morgan Freeman, and Dan Aykroyd), Miss Daisy has a hard time allowing her driver, who was hired by her son, to help her. She sees herself as being so independent, but she has gotten to the point where she needs to be interdependent. She needs a little help in order to maintain her life and her lifestyle. The story shows how difficult that journey is, and it takes a long time before she can graciously receive the help offered. At the end of the movie, Miss Daisy, now being cared for in an assisted living center, chooses her driver instead of her son as the one with whom she wants to visit. Her driver seems to listen and hear and understand her situation far better than her son.

When I was chaplain in the retirement community, I had an experience that exemplifies the hard knocks of trying to learn how to receive advice and guidance from an older person. Actually, the story starts when I was a new missionary in Korea trying to learn the Korean language. I thought that the best thing this brand-new missionary could do was to spend some time with a woman who had spent forty years in Korea and learn from her about what it was like to be a missionary in Korea. She invited me for a weekend, and as we talked I shared how difficult it was for me to try to learn the Korean language. I asked her why I should learn Korean anyway, since most Koreans knew a lot of English. She looked at me squarely in the eye and answered, "If you are going to communicate with these people, don't you think you should learn their language?" This gift of grace was hard to receive by this new missionary. I did study the Korean language, and although I was not and am not a linguist, I learned enough to say those things I needed to in Korean.

Thirty years later I was a seminary student doing an intern year in the retirement community, and here was that same woman from Korea, at the age of ninety-six, living in the independent living section, with the responsibility of "taking care" of all the other residents. When it came time for my first sermon, I practiced in front of the mirror, and had every body movement and facial expression in mind as the time came to preach the sermon. I threw myself into making this sermon the best that I could do. There were about fifty people present to hear this first sermon from the new chaplain. My ninety-six-year-old friend sat on the back row, listening intently.

When it was over, most of the people came and shook my hand, patted me on the back, and complimented me on my delivery, saying how happy they were to have me as their chaplain. When everyone else was gone, my friend approached me. Before she could say anything I asked, "How did you like my sermon?" As she had done thirty years earlier, she looked me squarely in the eye and said with determination, "If you are going to be a preacher, don't you think you should learn to preach?" I was dumbfounded! Shattered! Again, that grace was hard to receive!

My immediate reaction was to feel angry, even devastated. I had worked so hard to make it the perfect sermon. However, when I recovered I said, "I accept that challenge. Every Friday before I preach, I want to meet with you and go over my sermon, and every Monday after I preach, I want to meet with you and hear your critique." She agreed to the plan, and was faithful in her attention to the plan for the next six months or so.

I went to see her one day and found that she was in the hospital. When I located her room, she was in the hospital bed, looking very weak and tired. I asked if she had made a decision she had not told me about. She answered, "Yes. I came home from Korea in my mid-sixties thinking I would live a couple of years and then go to be with the Lord. But here I am at ninety-six, still here. It's time for me to go home." She died the next day. She didn't live long enough to see me graduate from seminary, where I won the annual preaching award. My preaching success was all because of this gracious, determined woman who knew how to give tough grace, and I had a hard lesson in how to receive that kind of grace.

WHAT DIFFERENCE DOES IT MAKE?

Some theological issues raised in this psalm bear some scrutiny:
1. On what does the psalmist base his assumption that he has

to beg for God not to cast him off and not to forsake him? From the psalmist's life experience of the faithfulness of God, why might he assume that at this time in his life God might forget him or deliberately cast him away?

2. At times in the psalm there are glimpses of bargaining. When my mother was facing surgery for breast cancer many years ago, I found myself engaging in some bargaining with God. At the time I was in the throes of making a decision about whether to go to seminary or to remain in what was then my position as a missionary recruiter. I went to the church the night before her surgery to an empty sanctuary, and I prayed to God that if God would bring my mother through this cancer episode, I would go to seminary and never look back. This was almost twenty years ago, and my mother is still with us at the age of ninety-two. I did indeed go to seminary to prepare myself for older adult ministry, and I never looked back! The psalmist borders on saying something like, "God, I have praised you and served you. You are a great God, you do wonderful things, and I have lived my life praising you. I look forward to a future of telling people of your might and power. Now, how about helping me out by rescuing me from my enemies and helping me through my present difficulties?" How do you respond to this idea?

3. The psalmist focuses more on the positive than on the negative. At the end of the psalm he focuses entirely upon his praise of God and calls on the whole earth to sing God's praises. How do you account for this magnificent ending to the psalm, in view of all the struggles, illnesses, criticism from enemies, and other calamities that he mentions previously?

PUTTING IT ALL TOGETHER
AND BRINGING IT HOME

One of the clearest messages in Psalm 71 has to do with telling the stories, the growing up stories as well as the growing older stories. The psalmist tells stories of the struggles and anguish of his older life and his younger life, as well as the joyful and peaceful times. We get a clear picture of how it was to be an older person in that day.

Here is an older person suffering from some kind of illness that has brought him near to death. As if this is not enough, there are people who are plotting against him, even using his ill-ness as an occasion to humiliate him and cause him great inner turmoil. I have experienced this kind of humiliation during an illness, demonstrating that the psalmist is in touch not only with the reality of his day, but also with modern times. The hu-man experience is a common experience.

In the modern world, perhaps the most dreaded loss is that of independence, of becoming dependent on others. Yet the psalmist writes of his dependence upon God since his birth; he sees such dependence not as a sign of his worthlessness or uselessness, but as the good gift of a gracious God.

Therefore, a message of this psalm might be a call to tell our stories—to tell of the youthful years of many struggles held up by the grace of a loving God, and of the later years and how it is to grow older. How are younger people to learn how to grow older gracefully and positively unless older people both provide the model and tell their stories? Conversely, how can older peo-ple learn to live in a rapidly changing world without the help of younger people, who learn computers and all the other modern technologies almost from birth? Perhaps for older adults it is in looking back that strength and perspective are gained in order to face an unknown future, and to reconfirm the blessed assur-ance that God will never cast out or forsake. For younger people, perhaps it is in looking forward through the eyes of the older persons that they can gain a perspective on what it means to live positively in the later years.

Some questions to ponder:

1. What is the message of Psalm 71 for your life?
2. In your own life, how might your memory of God's faith-fulness, rather than your memory of your "enemies" and their criticisms and hurtfulness, make a difference?
3. What connections do you make in your life between mem-ory and faith, between your past experiences of God's faith-fulness and your ability to trust God and affirm God's continued care over you in the present and in the future?
4. Have you ever prayed for and received deliverance from some experience in your life, when God intervened and set things right? Did you acknowledge that this was God's do-

ing and reflect on the meaning of that act, or did you go on with life without further reflection?

5. As Psalm 71 progresses from the psalmist's telling stories of his depression, anguish, fear, and anger, to his moving on to the praise of God and then to promises about what he will do in the future to praise God, something interesting happens. It seems that as the psalmist tells his story of the struggles and of the faithfulness of God, his faith reaches new heights in the latter portions of the psalm. In your own life, as you tell stories of your experience of God's faithfulness during struggles in your life, has your faith become clearer?

6. Have you ever bargained with God, promising that you would do something if God would see you through a crisis? How did that work?

7. After studying Psalm 71, what is the role of older persons that is set forth by the psalmist in verse 18? What prevents us from adopting that role for our own lives?

HELPS FOR GROUP STUDY

A. Begin the session by reading Psalm 71 from the NRSV. Then read the psalm one verse at a time from the different translations. Discuss the differences in translations, noting those that seem significant to the overall meaning.

B. Make a list of the struggles the psalmist mentions throughout the psalm.

C. Make a list of the ways in which God has been present in the life of the psalmist throughout his life.

D. Identify key words, images, or phrases that seem significant to the group, and ask why they are significant.

E. Discuss what the psalmist was saying to the readers of his day.

F. Discuss theological and personal issues raised by the psalmist, and add any others that are identified by the study group.

G. Explore what might be the message of Psalm 71 to readers in the modern world.

H. Help the participants to identify the message of Psalm 71 for their lives in their present circumstances.

I. What is the role of older adults in the modern world that is suggested by the psalmist? If you were to choose to make this your role for the rest of your life, how would you go about it?

J. What will you choose as your role in life for the rest of your life?

Notes

1. Jimmy Carter, *The Virtues of Aging* (New York: Ballatine Books, 1998), 48.
2. *The Interpreter's Bible,* vol. 4 (Nashville: Abingdon Press, 1955), 373.
3. Ibid., 378.
4. W. O. E. Oesterley, *The Psalms* (London: SPCK, 1959), 336.
5. *Interpreter's Bible,* 4:378.
6. Robert Davidson, *The Vitality of Worship: A Commentary on the Book of Psalms* (Grand Rapids: Wm. B. Eerdmans Publishing Co., 1998), 223.
7. Oesterley, *Psalms,* 240.
8. A. A. Anderson, *Psalms,* The New Century Bible Commentary, vol. 1 (Grand Rapids: Wm. B. Eerdmans Publishing Co. and London: Marshall, Morgan & Scott Publishing, 1972), 329.
9. *Interpreter's Bible,* 4:375.
10. *The Oxford Dictionary of Current English* (Oxford and New York: Oxford University Press, 1996), 694.
11. Anderson, *Psalms,* 329.
12. *The New Interpreter's Bible,* vol. 4 (Nashville: Abingdon Press, 1996), 961.

Chapter 7

Psalm 51
HOW CAN I BE RECONCILED TO ALL THAT I AM?

The Psalms are the oldest prayers in the Judeo-Christian tradition. . . . They are a lexicon of the human condition. . . . They assure us that our own hopes and fears, desires and emotions are just like the rest of the human condition.

—Joan Chittister

INTRODUCTION

Una Kroll has said, "One of the privileges of growing older is being able to look backwards and forwards at the same time."[1] As we grow older, sometimes it is easier to look backward than to look forward. Therefore, we choose to look back and think of the "good old days," a time when life seemed better than it does at the present time. We tend to look backward through rose-colored glasses, however, and we deceive ourselves into thinking that all was well. Indeed, there is another side to looking back. If we are truly honest in remembering those days, we sometimes can see another picture, one of failures and bad judgments that result in a sense of failure. We can look back on our lives and cry out, "If only I had . . . ," and come to retirement age with feelings of failure and worthlessness, asking "What was my life worth?"

Psalm 51 speaks to people who feel the need to remember the past, to feel sorrow for lost opportunities, broken relationships, and wrong decisions, and to be in communication with God concerning those pains and disappointments. Most of us have not sinned in the same manner as David when (and if) he wrote this prayer for repentance and confession. However, few of us can claim a clean slate for ourselves. Most of us have some pain that still remains with us in our later years about which we do need to communicate with God.

The need for reconciliation occurs when there is recognition of separation where there should be unity, distance where there should be closeness. Most often we think of a need for reconciliation where wrongdoing has occurred. One of the most pervasive roots of the need for reconciliation is wrongdoing in action or thought, in commission or omission. But there are other roots that need to be considered. For example, in a highly mobile society, with families and friends separated by long distances, breaches occur almost by accident. The intention was never there, but the effort was never really made. The usual sending of birthday cards and notes of encouragement, as well as the telephone calls to touch base are lost in the busyness of the modern world. This is not intentional, but it happens.

All of these can result in separation from individuals and separation from God. At the same time, something inside the individual gets separated as well. Perhaps the greatest task an individual faces in reconciliation is not so much owning up to whatever it was that resulted in the separation, admitting it, and seeking restoration, but turning it loose and moving on. This means accepting that it has occurred, that "I am not a perfect human being, that I have owned it and sought restoration with anyone or anything it may have affected, but now it is time to move on and live without the weight of it." This requires taking responsibility for oneself, one's actions, and one's future.

Clearly this psalm is about a wrong deed, a deed that affected another, and in affecting another deeply affected the psalmist's relationship with God. The psalmist owns up to this deed and seeks God's help in coming to terms with it and with the need to move on: "Create in me a clean heart, O God, and put a new and right spirit within me" (v. 10).

WHAT DOES THE PSALM SAY?

Psalm 51

> Have mercy on me, O God,
>   according to your steadfast love;
>   according to your abundant mercy
>   blot out my transgressions.

Wash me thoroughly from my iniquity,
  and cleanse me from my sin.
For I know my transgressions,
  and my sin is ever before me.
Against you, you alone, have I sinned,
  and done what is evil in your sight,
so that you are justified in your sentence
  and blameless when you pass judgment.
Indeed, I was born guilty,
  a sinner when my mother conceived me.
You desire truth in the inward being;
  therefore teach me wisdom in my secret heart.
Purge me with hyssop, and I shall be clean;
  wash me, and I shall be whiter than snow.
Let me hear joy and gladness;
  let the bones that you have crushed rejoice.
Hide your face from my sins,
  and blot out all my iniquities.
Create in me a clean heart, O God,
  and put a new and right spirit within me.
Do not cast me away from your presence,
  and do not take your holy spirit from me.
Restore to me the joy of your salvation,
  and sustain in me a willing spirit.
Then I will teach transgressors your ways,
  and sinners will return to you.
Deliver me from bloodshed, O God,
  O God of my salvation,
  and my tongue will sing aloud of your deliverance.
O Lord, open my lips,
  and my mouth will declare your praise.
For you have no delight in sacrifice;
  if I were to give a burnt offering, you would not be
    pleased.
The sacrifice acceptable to God is a broken spirit;
  a broken and contrite heart, O God, you will not
    despise.
Do good to Zion in your good pleasure;
  rebuild the walls of Jerusalem,

> then you will delight in right sacrifices,
>   in burnt offerings and whole burnt offerings;
>   then bulls will be offered on your altar.

The date of Psalm 51 cannot be known for sure. Although history says that David wrote the psalm, A. A. Anderson indicates that the ideas found are "more related to the concepts of the seventh and sixth centuries B.C.E. than to the thought of any earlier period."[2] This was clearly a time in Israel's life when prophets were warning the people of their separation from God. It was written at a time when people were acutely aware of their actions. There were prophets of the time saying, "If you do this, the following will result. However, if you turn around and do it differently, God has another future." It was open-ended.

According to James Mays, the language in Psalm 51 bears a striking likeness to Jeremiah, Ezekiel, and chapters 40–55 of Isaiah. "It was probably a liturgical text for the service that involved some kind of penitence, perhaps even the Day of Atonement."[3] It would seem that this psalm was for use in corporate worship by individuals, much like our own hymns. For example, when we sing "Amazing Grace" we individually personalize the hymn; but more than that, we identify our life and faith situation with the text. There are many hymns written by hymn writers about their own situation that invite others to resonate. It is possible that Psalm 51 was about a particular situation; it is entitled "A Psalm of David, when the prophet Nathan came to him, after he had gone in to Bathsheba." Whether this psalm really is rooted in a historical incident is immaterial. Even if the psalm were not actually written by David, it is certainly a realistic portrayal of the meaning of sin by a person who was deeply disturbed about his wrongdoing.[4] The circumstances are universal as well as specific. They describe a yearning for reconciliation, for the mending of a separation that has occurred within and without between individuals and between individuals and God.

WHAT DOES THE PSALM MEAN?

Perhaps the meaning of the psalm would be made clearer by looking at some of the key verses.

1. "Have mercy on me, O God, according to your steadfast

love" (v. 1) denotes an urgency and intensity on the part of the psalmist. Davidson points out that "this is an appeal which has its roots not in anything the psalmist can offer in self-justification, but solely in what he believes to be the essential character of God, summed up in the words, 'steadfast love' (5:7) and 'abundant mercy' or compassion, the kind of love that a mother has for the child she bears."[5]

The psalmist pleads with God for mercy. He writes from his position of severe agony, asking in several different and graphic ways for God to rid him of his wrongdoing. In verses 1–2 the writer introduces three words for sin—*transgressions, iniquity,* and *sin,* and then identifies their counterparts in the next few verses with "blot out . . . wash me . . . cleanse me."[6] However, I have wondered sometimes if we don't at times confuse forgiveness with the notion that a particular sin has truly been "blotted out."

I have wondered if starting afresh, as we often say, harbors a secret belief that the clock has been put back, allowing us to go forward as if it never happened. On the contrary, we always have to live with the consequences of our wrongdoings, even though forgiven. Too often we leave it all up to God; we ask for forgiveness, and expect God to "fix it." However, there is restitution as well as restoration. We have a responsibility to make amends, and then to leave it behind and move on. It is true that sometimes the pain is so deep and so longstanding that making amends is very difficult if not impossible. When this happens all are the losers.

2. Verses 3–4 read: "For I know my transgressions, and my sin is ever before me. Against you, you alone, have I sinned." Once we have engaged in wrongdoing it is always with us. We may be able to push it aside for a short time, but it continues to emerge and plague us. Although the sin of the psalmist has hurt other human beings, the concern of the psalmist is his relationship with God, assuming that if his relationship with God is put right he can deal with the sin against another human being. However, if his relationship with God is not put right, then all is lost because it is in relationship with God that we humans can get a clear picture of the sin committed. This verse has caused some conflict because of the fact that although the sin is against God, it has also probably hurt others.

An issue that we should discuss in connection with these

verses is our feelings of guilt. What do we do with the feelings of guilt that result from wrongdoing? How can we bear to have our failures seen by those around us? How can we dare to face God even in repentance? We want to run and hide, not face the world, to somehow get rid of the gnawing pains inside us, and to rewrite history by saying it never happened. When the psalmist comes to the end of his rope, when he has faced the worst within himself with complete honesty, when he has bared his soul before God in repentance, the turnaround begins and hope revives once more that perhaps life can go on, renewed, clean, and filled with "a right spirit within me."

3. "Indeed, I was born guilty, a sinner when my mother conceived me." Verse 5 also raises some interesting points and some difficult and complex issues about the nature of the human person, the nature of God, and the human predicament. The psalmist seems to indicate that the very nature of our humanity means we are born in separation from God. What the psalmist seems to be relating to is that although we don't know what "truth in the inward being" (v. 6) means, he has grasped that it is something internal rather than external, and something that the psalmist needs God to bring about.

4. This leads us to verse 6: "You desire truth in the inward being." Most translations have a footnote to indicate that the meaning of the Hebrew for "in the inward being" is uncertain. Therefore, it is translated in various ways—"in the inward being" (NRSV), "in the inner parts" (NIV), "in the secret place" (JB), but there is no indication as to what these translations mean in the context of the whole passage. *The New Interpreter's Bible* says that "verse 6 suggests that sin is not the final word about humanity. God desires not sinfulness but faithfulness."[7] Davidson's interpretation of this difficult phrase is "what is not visible on the surface," and he understands the phrase "secret heart" to mean "what is there at the very core of someone's life." He says, "There can be no self-achieved piety or forgiveness."[8]

5. Verse 10 is perhaps the most familiar and most quoted of all the verses in Psalm 51. These words form a climax to the psalm. After going through all the anguish of repentance, owning up to sinful ways, and asking for forgiveness, the tide has turned and the climax is to give the psalmist another chance: Clean my slate

and let me start over as if this did not happen. The author is "not asking for transformation, but for a new creation."[9]

6. In verses 13–14 ("Then I will teach transgressors your ways"), when the writer feels that he has been cleansed by the wonderful grace of forgiveness and now has a "right spirit" within, it is only natural that he wants to use that experience to share with others who are going through similar circumstances, and help them turn back to God. "This speaker who has utterly relinquished self to God dares now to look ahead, beyond the emptiness of the moment."[10]

7. Verses 15–17 are also intriguing: "O Lord, open my lips, and my mouth will declare your praise. For you have no delight in sacrifice; if I were to give a burnt offering, you would not be pleased. The sacrifice acceptable to God is a broken spirit; a broken and contrite heart, O God, you will not despise." Although some commentators ask about the discrepancy between these verses and verses 18–19 on the issue of whether or not God delights in sacrifice, there does not seem to me to be a conflict. The meaning seems clear enough that going through the motions, such as giving sacrifices and burnt offerings, does not make any difference, but that what is required is a change inside the person. This idea fits with the prophetic period in which this psalm might have occurred. The people of Israel needed to accept the responsibility for the religious and social situations they had created. It was no good going through the motions. The people had to own what was happening within their own hearts, and only then could what God intended be used aright.

We do this with forgiveness. We say "blot it out, take it away, make it like it never happened." But the reality of our creatureliness and time-bound nature is that it doesn't work that way. We must live with the consequences of what we have done. What God wants is for persons to reverse the course of action that has brought about separation with God, and with a sense of repentance come to God totally, submit to God completely, and receive God's grace and forgiveness. The task is to be reconciled to who I am and to all that has happened that made me who I am.

The themes in Psalm 51 are obvious: anguish over wrongdoings, confession, forgiveness, renewal, restoration of relationship, and promises to teach others about God's ways and to give praise to God. Are there other themes that need to be noted?

By way of summary, the author calls on God to treat him with mercy, followed by his confession of a terrible wrong, a prayer for cleansing and renewal, and a promise to "sing aloud of your deliverance," and to praise God for forgiveness and restoration.

WHAT DIFFERENCE DOES IT MAKE?

This psalm is not of the usual kind of psalms, especially of lament that are fitted with complaints about how God is mistreating the writer, or how the psalmist is lashing out at God because of feelings of abandonment. Rather, the total focus of this writing is on the sinfulness of the self. It is a very intense hymn, and beautiful in its eloquence and humility. Therefore, the message of the psalm assumes that God is a God of love who is willing to forgive and restore, and who yearns for this to happen when there is separation as a consequence of wrongdoing. When true repentance comes, along with confession and humility, God forgives and restores, and delights in the renewal of the relationship.

There are a number of theological and personal issues raised in this psalm:

1. When does the sinner know that he or she is forgiven and restored in relationship with God? This is not addressed in the psalm. There is the assumption that God will forgive and all will be well. But the psalm does not talk about how the psalmist knew that he was forgiven.

2. There is the problem of saying "Against you, you alone, have I sinned" (v. 4), which leaves out the human beings who might have been the victims of the sin. Even when forgiveness comes, the results of the sin still remain. So the question is: How does forgiveness from God help in resolving the situation when the victims are still in pain?

3. Is there a conflict in the final verses when the psalmist is offering a prayer for Zion? He says plainly that sacrifices do not please God. But in his prayer he indicates that when Jerusalem is rebuilt, God will delight in "right sacrifices." If there is a conflict here, can it be resolved? If not, explain the meaning of the conflict.

PUTTING IT ALL TOGETHER
AND BRINGING IT HOME

As we grow older we look back to claim a sense that our lives have been worthwhile, that at least we accomplished something that was good, so that when we leave this world we leave it a little better place than it was when we entered. These remembrances help us find strength to face the crises of the present, to cherish where we are in our lives now, and to look forward to the future with a renewed sense of hope.

However, there is a downside to remembering. Several things can happen. We can be reminded of wrongdoings that have caused pain to family members, friends, or others. We can be reminded of broken relationships that once were cherished and treasured. We can rewrite our history to convince ourselves that the negative actions didn't really happen that way, or that they were not our fault, and revise our memories so that what happened is more acceptable.

By remembering, though, we can review the facts and reference points that establish the truth, and with God's help, we can face the truth about our lives. Through the facts and reference points we can reestablish a certain stability that can provide support through the present difficulties. Remembering the people and the events that molded our lives, we can renew a sense of identity, clarify our strengths, and discover a perspective on our lives that can bring a sense of progress toward a solid future.

The psalmist was in deep anguish over past sins. He came to God in repentance and humility, expecting God's grace of forgiveness and the restoration of his relationship with God. This same grace is available to us, but even more so now. Since these words were written, something else has happened. Jesus the Christ came to show us what it means to live a life in right relationship with God, with other human beings and with ourselves. In doing this, he was killed because of the sinfulness in the world. But he rose again to demonstrate that the power of God overcomes the sin of the world. "For God so loved the world that [God] gave [the] only Son, so that everyone who believes in him may not perish but may have eternal life" (John 3:16).

The other thing that the psalmist did was to vow before God

to "teach transgressors your ways." In other words, the psalmist will tell his story of God's deliverance from the anguish he had felt because of his wrongdoing. Older adults are encouraged to tell their stories of deliverance from all kinds of crisis experiences, and of God's faithfulness throughout their lives.

HELPS FOR GROUP STUDY

A. Read the psalm one verse at a time with all participating who wish to do so. Discuss the differences in the various translations.

B. Ask the group what they think was going on in the life of the psalmist when he wrote the psalm.

C. Discuss the key words, images, or phrases that give a clue to clarification of the feelings, such as the various words used for sin and the different verbs used to describe what the psalmist wants from God.

D. Discuss whether or not the concept of sin is different now from what it was when the psalm was written. What is sin? When does behavior become sin rather than an error in judgment?

E. It is a human trait to seek justification for actions by explaining the circumstances, defending ourselves, blaming someone else or the situation, or trying to "look good" in the eyes of others. Why did the psalmist not do this, instead throwing himself on the mercy of God and begging for forgiveness without defense? Ask the group how they as individuals approach God when some act or experience has caused separation.

F. Lead the group in a discussion of guilt. Does guilt disappear when forgiveness is requested? What is the role of guilt in the whole process of repentance, seeking and receiving forgiveness, and in moving ahead with life?

G. Close the session by asking the group to read the psalm again individually and silently, claiming it for themselves to the extent they can.

H. End the session with prayer.

Notes

1. Una Kroll, *Growing Older* (Glasgow: William Collins Sons & Co., 1988), 52.

2. A. A. Anderson, *Psalms,* The New Century Bible Commentary, vol. 1 (Grand Rapids: Wm. B. Eerdmans Publishing Co. and London: Marshall, Morgan & Scott Publishing, 1972), 389.

3. James L. Mays, *Psalms,* Interpretation: A Bible Commentary for Teaching and Preaching (Louisville, KY.: John Knox Press, 1994), 199.

4. *The Interpreter's Bible,* vol. 4 (Nashville: Abingdon Press, 1955), 267.

5. Robert Davidson, *The Vitality of Worship A Commentary on the Book of Psalms* (Grand Rapids: Wm. B. Eerdmans Publishing Co., 1998), 167.

6. Ibid.

7. *The New Interpreter's Bible,* vol. 4 (Nashville: Abingdon Press, 1996), 886.

8. Davidson, *Vitality of Worship,* 169.

9. Anderson, *Psalms,* 398.

10. Walter Brueggemann, *The Message of the Psalms: A Theological Commentary,* Old Testament Studies (Minneapolis: Augsburg Publishing House, 1984), 101.

Chapter 8

Psalm 23
CALM ASSURANCE IN THE MIDST OF DARK VALLEYS

Psalm 23 remains the best loved of all biblical passages. The living have lived by it, the dying have died by it; it is the priceless possession of the people of God, and never fails to speak to wherever people are on the journey of life.

—Richard L. Morgan

INTRODUCTION

Psalm 23 is perhaps the most familiar, the most loved, the most memorized, and the most quoted of all the psalms. In past generations, children recited it almost as soon as they could talk. Older people die with it as their last words. It is used at funerals to bring comfort to grieving families and recited at family reunions to bind them together. In many homes in the South, Psalm 23 hangs on walls, framed in all its many forms: embroidered, knitted, painted in oil, drawn by professional calligraphers, hewn out of wood or copper, or scrawled by a child. A little girl once recited Psalm 23 with a new twist. She said, "The Lord's my shepherd; that's all I want." She said more than she realized.

Psalm 23 is profound, yet simple. It is enchanting and down-to-earth. George A. F. Knight has said, "It expresses more vividly than any other portion of scripture the individual's private experience of God's grace."[1] Walter Brueggemann writes, "It is almost pretentious to comment on this psalm. The grip it has on biblical spirituality is deep and genuine. It is such a simple statement that it can bear its own witness without comment."[2]

What is there about this psalm that makes it so beloved? What human need does it meet that causes it to be so widely memorized, recited, and pondered? In its sweetness and simplicity is there a message that has been missed? Does the psalm encourage an unrealistic view of the world? How can persons living in the computer age, far removed from the lonely life of a shepherd, understand or in any way link up with the shepherd image? Does the psalm have a special message for people in the later years of life, or is their attachment to it purely sentimental? With these questions in mind, read the psalm and ponder its meaning.

WHAT DOES THE PSALM SAY?

Psalm 23 (RSV)

> The LORD is my shepherd, I shall not want;
>   he makes me lie down in green pastures.
> He leads me beside still waters;
>   he restores my soul.
> He leads me in paths of righteousness
>   for his name's sake.
> Even though I walk through the valley of the shadow of
>   death,
>   I fear no evil;
> for thou art with me;
>   thy rod and thy staff,
>   they comfort me.
> Thou preparest a table before me
>   in the presence of my enemies;
> thou anointest my head with oil,
>   my cup overflows.
> Surely goodness and mercy shall follow me
>   all the days of my life;
> and I shall dwell in the house of the LORD
>   for ever.

I grew up on a farm in the state of Georgia. During my teenage years and later, my father was in the business of raising white-faced Hereford cattle. One time my father asked me to round up the cows and move them into the adjacent pasture. I went to the pasture, got behind the herd of cattle, and tried everything I could think of to drive them through the narrow gate into the other pasture. I shouted, prodded, punched, and became very frustrated. The harder I tried the more determined were the cows not to go where I wanted them to go. I was a total failure. Then I watched my father do it. He walked very calmly into the pasture, called to them softly, rattled the feed sack, and all the cows immediately headed toward him. He then walked slowly through the narrow gate, and the cows followed him, every one without hesitation.

I thought, "Oh, I can do that!" So the next time my father asked me to take care of this duty I took the feed sack with me, called softly to the cows, and again they totally ignored my presence. One or two of them may have looked up out of idle curiosity, but otherwise I was totally ignored. You see, they knew my father. They knew his voice. They knew that he was the one who took care of them, fed them, and provided fresh water for them. They would follow him anywhere. My father was always ahead, leading them to the best place for them, just as the shepherd did for the sheep.

This seems to me to be the message of Psalm 23. The Lord, in caring for us, is like my father caring for his cattle or a shepherd caring for his sheep. The sheep know the shepherd, trust the shepherd, and know that the shepherd will lead them to the places that are best for them. In verses 1–4 the shepherd leads the sheep to a place with plenty of water and green grass, and guides them safely through the dark valleys, always in the path that gives life and comfort. In verses 5–6, the image changes to that of a host who takes care of the needs of the guests at the banquet, granting them hospitality in the present and the assurance of presence in the future.

In seeking to determine what a psalm is saying, sometimes it is helpful to explore when it was written, under what circumstances, and by whom it was written. Scholars are not sure of the authorship of Psalm 23. However, some facts are known. The words, "A Psalm of David," printed at the beginning, do not necessarily refer to authorship. They indicate only that the psalm was taken from the early psalters gathered together under the name of David. The words could mean that the psalms were written by David, or were simply in David's collection. The traditional belief, however, is that King David himself did indeed write Psalm 23.

The author is obviously enjoying the peace of mind that comes from a firm trust in God (vv. 1–2). The author's maturity is evident in verses 4–5, a seasoning that comes from having experienced struggle and fought many battles. In his older years he has found intimate communion with God, with an accompanying inner peace and strength that sustains him. So the author could have been David the musician, the poet, the shepherd boy, or the king who sins, repents, and asks forgiveness. If so, he could have been looking back to his childhood days as a shepherd, guiding his sheep, and to his kingly days as a host at table. In the end, however, authorship cannot be known for sure.

Circumstances seem to have been peaceful and prosperous when the psalm was written, in contrast to the trials, suffering, and sorrow of the exile. The image of the shepherd gives no guidance as to date, since the image of Yahweh as shepherd is found as early as the story of Jacob. Therefore, the date is unknown and only assumptions can be made. If it was written by David it could have been written between 970 and 961, during the latter years of his life.

The placement of Psalm 23 between Psalm 22 and Psalm 24 seems significant. Psalm 22 is a psalm of individual lament, a moving portrayal of the suffering of one who is isolated and torn by some affliction. The psalmist cries out the ultimate cry of despair: "My God, my God, why have you forsaken me?" Psalm 24, on the other hand, is a glorious hymn of exaltation. With the ultimate image of calm assurance in Psalm 23 between the two extremes, there is a progression from utter despair and desolation to a picture of the Lord as caring shepherd, and finally to a magnificent celebration and praise of God, describing how such a God should be praised in true worship.

It is helpful sometimes in exploring what a psalm is saying to read the different translations. Frequently, some of the Hebrew words are interpreted differently in different translations. For example, in the King James Version verse 4 is translated "Yea, though I walk through the valley of the shadow of death, I will fear no evil: for thou art with me; thy rod and thy staff they comfort me." However, the word for "death" in Hebrew is not found in Psalm 23. Therefore, the New Revised Standard Version translates the Hebrew to read, "Even though I walk through the darkest valley," with a reference note indicating the traditional translation "valley of the shadow of death." The Good News Bible translates it "deepest darkness." The Jerusalem Bible uses the word "gloom."

Whatever the original meaning of the Hebrew word, the danger of death was certainly present in the mountains of Palestine, and so the valleys of deepest darkness, whether literal or metaphorical, brought fear and anxiety. As older persons who sometimes experience those valleys, we can certainly identify with the significant change that takes place immediately following these words. When speaking of deep darkness, the author changes from speaking of the shepherd in the third person ("he") to speaking of him in the second person ("you" or "thou"), perhaps emphasizing the need for closeness in the midst of danger, fear, and anxiety.

Another way to decipher what the psalm says is to read it verse by verse, looking for themes, images, and patterns.

"The LORD is my shepherd, I shall not want" literally means that since the Lord is a constant, caring presence, the psalmist believes he will lack for nothing. This is perhaps the most difficult of all the verses to interpret, but also perhaps the most comforting. It raises the question: What about those persons who are believers and yet are persecuted or are hungry for food or homeless, and yet have nothing? The verse sounds as though God will grant our every need. Yet in the world in which we live we know this is not true. What then does it mean? Is it speaking of the material or the spiritual or both?

Verse 2 ("He makes me lie down in green pastures. He leads me beside still waters") literally says that he causes me to rest in meadows of green tender grass, and that he gently guides me to rest in a camp beside the water. As with the sheep, the world we live in is a world of deserts and droughts, and there is nothing available that will satisfy the deepest longings of the soul. As with the sheep, we also cannot rest until we are free from fear, from tensions and stress, and from the physical needs of food, water, and loving care. The shepherd leads the sheep to the tender green meadows, where there is peace and rest with plenty of food and water. And so it is with God. God is always present with us, always with our best interests at heart, and always looking for the best places for us to find peace, rest, and satisfaction.

In verse 3 ("He restores my soul. He leads me in paths of righteousness for his name's sake"), the Hebrew word for *soul* means "the living being," or "life principle." The closest translation may be "he restores life within me." The rest of the verse may be saying that he guides me in paths that are right for me because it is in the nature of God to do so; this is who God is. At any rate, the idea seems to be that God continues to refresh the life of the psalmist, has guided the psalmist into paths that lead to the sources that restore life and peace, and has kept the psalmist from paths that would lead otherwise.

In verse 4 ("Even though I walk through the valley of the shadow of death, I fear no evil; for thou art with me; thy rod and thy staff, they comfort me"), the meaning is very comforting. It means that even if I experience the deepest darkness imaginable, there is no need to be afraid, because God promises to be with me, to protect me, to comfort me, and to make me secure. The psalmist has not been protected from suffering and evil in the world. He too has been through troubles, but his close communion with God becomes real to him when he thinks of those times of distress. In shifting to the second person here, the psalmist turns his testimony into a prayer, addressing God directly. It is as if the writer remembered the distress experienced, and wanted to emphasize the need of closeness even more. The psalmist points out that even during those times of darkness God did not forsake him. God showed unconditional love for him, especially in times of danger and loneliness. Because of his looking back at those times and seeing how God has been his guide, his protector, and his comforter, the psalmist can face the future without fear and with confidence, no matter what comes.

The literal translation of verse 5 from the Hebrew text says that "you prepare a feast for me and I am secure even in front of all my enemies, that you welcome me with favor as an honored guest and you completely fill me with happiness." With the shift of the scene comes the feeling of blessing and joy to be able to take part in the feast as a guest of God (see Psalm 15:1). In the midst of his joy at the table, the psalmist realizes that even those who are against him cannot spoil his happiness in the presence of God. That is, when in God's presence, the joy is so great that the bitter experiences of life can be endured.

The word *cup* is significant. It speaks of more than just a container to hold liquid. *The Interpreter's Dictionary of the Bible* explains, "The cup was widely used in figurative language in the Old Testament, symbolic of the kind of life experience which God, the host, pours out for God's people."[3] There were many uses for the symbolism of the cup. For the righteous, the cup indicated the blessing of God, as in Psalm 23; for the wicked, the cup indicated the wrath of God (see Psalm 11:6). In the New Testament, there is the cup from the Lord's Supper found in the Gospels, and the words of Jesus in the Garden of Gethsemane: "Remove this cup from me" (Luke 22:42). So the meaning is far deeper and richer than simply a container. It has to do with the whole of life experience. The verb *runs over* could mean to be saturated, satisfied, or having something in great abundance. The meaning here may be that so plentiful are the blessings of God that the psalmist is saturated with joy and gladness.

Verse 6 ("Surely goodness and mercy shall follow me all the days of my life; and I shall dwell in the house of the LORD for ever") is particularly difficult to translate. However, it seems to be saying that the psalmist knows that God's goodness and steadfast love will be with him all the rest of his days, and that the psalmist will keep on returning to the house of God and sharing in its worship as long as he lives. The psalm has moved from short and profound sentences to longer sentences to a climax of joy, faith, and hope for an eternal presence with God. The basis of the joy is that God's goodness and mercy will be part of his life for the rest of his life. The psalmist looks toward the time when he will be with God, not only as a guest, but as a member of God's household in the most intimate and unbroken fellowship. For us, the meaning is the same. In the midst of the struggles through the dark valleys, as we face our own enemies, both internal and external, we know God's presence with us, caring for us. We can look toward the time when we, too, will be with God, not only as a guest, but as a member of God's household, experiencing close and unbroken communion with our Creator.

Davidson explains the meaning this way: "To the house of the Lord, to God's dwelling place in the midst of his people, he shall return again and again to renew his vitality through joining in worship and sharing a vision with the people of God. Theology divorced from worship is arid; life devoid of worship has limited horizons."[4]

WHAT DOES THE PSALM MEAN?

A number of theological issues are raised or addressed by Psalm 23. It might be helpful to ponder these issues in an effort to explore the meaning of the psalm. One of these issues is the matter of the providence of God and the problem of suffering. How can a loving God allow terrible things to happen in the lives of good people? Either God is without power to intervene, or chooses not to intervene. Neither of these descriptions fits the image of an all-powerful God who loves us. Perhaps the answer lies in Psalm 23:4, where the psalmist says plainly that there is no fear in the dark valleys because God is there with him, with all that is needed to bring comfort. This may include both "tough love" and "warm fuzzies," because the staff with the crook on the end was used not only to guide, but also to discipline.

A second theological issue has to do with the meaning of "I shall not want." How can there be abundance for some while the many remain in need? Is the psalmist referring only to spiritual needs—such as a yearning for God—as contrasted with physical needs—such as food, clothing, and shelter? Is there a message here for those who have things in abundance? Is there a message here for those who lack material things, but who are blessed with a close and satisfying walk with God?

A third theological issue to ponder concerns shepherding as a way of relating to other persons. How can the caring, guiding role of the shepherd be carried out in such a way as not to reduce to helpless sheep those for whom the shepherd cares? What was Jesus' model for relating, guiding, and caring for others?

In addition to the theological issues raised by Psalm 23, there are some intense personal issues that directly link up with the concerns of men and women in the later years of life. Who among us has not experienced the reality of fear in the midst of dark valleys, whether the basis of the fear is a serious illness, the death of a close family member, the loss of meaning in life, loneliness, or some other cause? Who among us does not have the need for permanency and security in the midst of the many transitions that come? Who among us does not have a need for companionship in the midst of ultimate human loneliness? Who among us has not experienced the reality of enemies, both internal and external, and experienced the dire need to be protected? Who among us does not have a need for future hope? We all experience these transitions, fears, insecurities, and times of loneliness at one time or another, and it is amazing that in these few verses of Psalm 23, the psalmist addresses all of these and more.

PUTTING IT ALL TOGETHER
AND BRINGING IT HOME

In studying this most beloved of all psalms, the question emerges as to why and how the image of the shepherd can have such deep meaning in the computer age among people so far removed from the shepherd's rod and staff. It would seem that this image is so powerful that it can ignore changing times, changing cultures, and changing careers. After all, this image of God as the shepherd of God's people graces the pages of the Bible in both the Old and New Testaments. In the Gospel of John, the image of the shepherd is applied to Jesus when he says, "I am the good shepherd." In this psalm, unlike most other psalms, there is no plea with God for assistance, no bargaining with God, no anger at God; there is only an affirmation of who God is and what God has done. It expresses complete confidence and assurance in the goodness and faithfulness of God, no matter what the circumstances.

This does not mean that the shepherd does not allow the sheep to move into dangerous areas, nor does the shepherd ensure that there are no enemies, only that in the midst of the danger or in the midst of insecurities, the sheep can feel protected, confident and secure. In *Psalms for the Journey,* Larry Kalajainen takes the thought a step further: "So this psalm is not only an expression of how any individual 'sheep' feels at any given moment. Rather, it is a confession that is at once public and historical; I confess God as my shepherd, not only because I have experienced God's care, but also because I belong to a community that has experienced God's shepherding care . . . that God's faithfulness to each individual sheep is intimately related to God's faithfulness to the whole flock."[5]

Therefore, we are not only individually connected to God and recipients of God's grace, faithfulness, and security, but we are also a part of a community of faith that has experienced the same shepherding of God that has been happening for thousands of years!

HELPS FOR GROUP STUDY

A. Read the psalm aloud in the group one verse at a time until all who want to read have an opportunity to do so. Because there are only six verses, this may require repeating the psalm several times. This is helpful since group members may read from different versions. It will become immediately obvious that there are significant differences in the translations.

B. Compare the different translations. Point out the major differences and discuss the significance of each.

C. Choose the key words, images, and concepts. For each one point out its significance. What does it teach about God, about human beings? Some examples of images would be "shepherd," "host," "meadows of green grass," and "goodness and mercy."

D. Identify themes in the psalm (e.g., need for companionship, fear of the valleys of darkness, assurance that God cares, hope for the future).

E. Invite individuals in the group to summarize the psalm.

F. Review the historical data.

G. Discussion starters:
   1. Think back in your life, and try to recover your earliest memory of Psalm 23. What did the psalm mean to you then? Were there other times in your life when Psalm 23 was significant to you?
   2. What do you believe was going on in the life of the psalmist at the time he wrote the psalm?
   3. What are your fears in your present situation?
   4. Who are your enemies?
   5. What is your source of hope?

      6. What does the psalm mean to you in your present circumstances?

      7. What message does the psalm have for you today?

H. Encourage group members to tell their stories, including both the joys and sorrows they have or may be experiencing.

I. End the study time by reading Psalm 23 from *Psalms Now,* a paraphrase by Leslie Brandt (St. Louis: Concordia Publishing House, 1974; revised in 1996).

Notes

1. George A. F. Knight, *Psalms,* vol. 1 of *The Daily Study Bible* (Philadelphia: Westminster Press, 1982), 115.

2. Walter Brueggemann, *The Message of the Psalms: A Theological Commentary,* Old Testament Studies (Minneapolis: Augsburg Publishing House, 1984), 154.

3. "Cup," *The Interpreter's Dictionary of the Bible* (Nashville: Abingdon Press, 1962), 748–49.

4. Robert Davidson, *The Vitality of Worship: A Commentary on the Book of Psalms* (Grand Rapids: Wm. B. Eerdmans Publishing Co., 1998), 85.

5. Larry R. Kalajainen, *Psalms for the Journey* (Nashville: Upper Room Books, 1996), 122.

Chapter 9

Psalm 131
I AM WHERE I WANT
TO BE AND THAT IS GOOD!

The Psalms speak as both poetry and praise.
Some of them are very great poems. But as
prayer, even the greatest poems are inadequate.
Pure prayer begins at the threshold of silence. . . .
The deeper the listening, the less we listen for,
until silence itself becomes the voice of God.
—Stephen Mitchell

INTRODUCTION

As we get older we look over our lives for things that have brought value and quality to life. We also become aware of those things we did that we wish we had not done, and of those things that we did not do that we wish we had done. In the process of sifting through these memories, many times we can find a peace that we have not known before. The stormy days of youth are over when we struggled for independence. The trauma of seeking our place in the working world, asserting and assuring our independence from parents as young adults, is long past. The responsibilities related to raising a family are behind us, and as we enter the later years of life we realize that we are indeed dependent human beings, and that we have been in deep need of God's guidance all of our lives. We find ourselves at a place of humility, peacefulness, and satisfaction with our lives. At some point, we learn about and accept that dependence is not a four-letter word, and we can find contentment in that knowledge.

Although some scholars say this psalm was definitely written by David, William Holladay offers an alternative theory that Psalm 131 may have been written by a woman. He follows German scholar Gottfried Quell, who put forth a strong argument that at least verses 1 and 2 were written by a woman. Quell's argument is that in those two verses there are statements of modesty and serenity, and that at the end of verse 2a, there is a strong pause. Holladay makes the point even stronger that the writer is female when he points out that verse 2b takes a different turn, using imagery that reveals clearly that the poem was written by a woman[1] "my soul is like the weaned child that is with me." Since the argument is so strong, and since it is such an intriguing challenge to think about this psalm being written by a woman, I will use feminine references for the author.

Holladay goes on to suggest that "one can assume that there would have been a specific experience of women in Israelite times that would have resonance with women's experience today, but unfortunately, that experience of Israelite women has left little written trace in the biblical record." He further indicates that "we have already noted the probability that Psalm 131 was written by a woman, but we have no assurance that the experience of women has left any direct trace in other psalms."[2]

The New Interpreter's Bible supports this idea: "V. 2 is striking because a straightforward translation of v. 2c suggests that the psalmist is almost certainly a woman."[3] Of course, the psalm could still have been written by David, or it could have been part of a collection of writings by the household of David. However, knowing the identity of the author is not necessary in order to experience the warmth, the humility, and the inspiration of the beautiful words of this poem in describing the situation of the writer, who, after experiencing some turmoil in her life, has found quiet and calm at last.

Weiser believes that this psalm "deserves to be classed with the most beautiful psalms of the Psalter."[4] With such words of praise concerning Psalm 131, it will be good to ponder this short and simple psalm, and seek out a message for our own day and lives.

WHAT DOES THE PSALM SAY?

Psalm 131

> O LORD, my heart is not lifted up,
>   my eyes are not raised too high;

I do not occupy myself with things
    too great and too marvelous for me.
But I have calmed and quieted my soul,
    like a weaned child with its mother;
    my soul is like the weaned child that is with me. [Or,
    my soul within me is like a weaned child.]
O Israel, hope in the LORD
    from this time on and forevermore.

WHAT DOES THE PSALM MEAN?

Artur Weiser observes that "the Hebrew words imply so much that they can be expressed adequately only by paraphrase." Therefore, we suggest that you read the paraphrase versions in the *Psalms* by Eugene H. Peterson[5] and *Psalms Now* by Leslie Brandt. These readings might help in the interpretation of the verses as we try to ponder the moods of these different versions alongside the NRSV. What is the difference in spirit of these three versions?

This is one of the shortest of the psalms, but it is filled with deep meaning. It might broaden the understanding of the psalm if we look at each verse individually.

Verse 1: "O LORD, my heart is not lifted up, my eyes are not raised too high." *The New Interpreter's Bible* points out that this verse refers to both internal matters (i.e., the author's heart) and external matters (i.e., the author's eyes), "that in both thought and deed, she has become humble."[6]

There is nothing in the verse that gives a hint as to the time or the situation of the author. However, we can surmise that she has had some experience that has turned her away from craving status, material things, and position, and has come to a place of deep humility. P. D. Miller, further supporting the idea that the author is a woman, points out that the phrases "great matters" and "things too wonderful" could indicate the "role restrictions placed upon women in the patriarchal structure of Israelite society." He further surmises that such a restriction "may account at least in part for the struggle implied in v. 2—that is, the woman's need to find a calmness of soul, a peace of mind and heart, that is denied her by her social setting."[7]

Brueggemann gives a slightly different view of who the writer is by pointing out that the person in the first verse is not prideful, arrogant, or full of himself, as other commentaries indicate. (Brueggemann assumes that the psalm has a male author.) On the contrary, the writer is saying he is innocent and has not thought too highly of himself, thus exhibiting a knowledge that a good relationship with God is not supposed to be "a relationship between equals, but is of subordination, submission and trust which the speaker gladly accepts."[8] However, Davidson has a different idea. He states that "vaulting ambition, pride, and meddling in affairs beyond his (her) ability and comprehension had once shaped his (her) life, but that calm and quietness have replaced restlessness and needless anxiety."[9] Whatever the true interpretation of the verse, there is the indication that the writer has come to terms with life and has found peace.

Verse 2: "But I have calmed and quieted my soul, like a weaned child with its mother; my soul is like the weaned child that is with me." A notation in the NRSV indicates an alternative translation for the last phrase: "my soul is like a weaned child." The indication here is that the groundswells of emotion have leveled, the mental and spiritual struggles are over, and at last the soul is calm and serene, just like a child that has been weaned and is happy just to be in the presence of the mother. Oesterley points out, "The comparison of the reposeful state of sublime self-abandonment to God with a child's unspoken trust in its mother's love and care is as touching as it is beautiful."[10]

This verse raises an obvious question: What happened that turned her around? If the psalmist was previously haughty, conceited, and ambitious, and then suddenly struggled through some trauma and came out with the peaceful and settled feelings described, how did that happen? Oesterley gives a hint when he notes that the first thing that happens is "that self-knowledge leads to confession, which implies repentance."[11]

Verse 3: "O Israel, hope in the LORD, from this time on and forevermore." Most scholars say this verse was not a part of the original psalm, but was added later. The purpose for adding it was to apply the teaching of the earlier part of the psalm to the image of Israel. The image included Israel's insisting on its own way, but then yielding in obedience to the faithfulness of God. "Unless there is submission, there will be no hope, for autonomy and self-sufficiency are finally postures of hopelessness in which free gifts are excluded and one is left to one's own resources. In this psalm, Israel is able to hope and to receive good gifts from this feeding God."[12] At any rate, the psalm ends on a hopeful note, with the author encouraging the readers to focus all hopes and expectations on the Lord. Such a focus is the secret to the calm and peaceful life.

Even if this verse was a later addition to the poem, it does seem an appropriate ending. In the scriptures the Israelites are sometimes referred to as a "stiff-necked people," perhaps referring to a tendency toward pride. Mays points out that "verse 2 prepares for and interprets verse 3. . . . [T]he image of the loving, comforting mother embracing her needy child portrays Israel's hope."[13]

Some themes in the psalm are obvious. For example, in verses 1–2, there is the theme of pride turning into humility, turmoil turning into calmness, chaos becoming quietness in the soul. It seems appropriate that Psalm 131 follows on the heels of Psalm 130. Psalm 130 is a penitential psalm in which the author tells how a soul that is repentant sought God, found God, and, as a result, found peace of soul. Psalm 131 picks up at that point and describes how it was before, and how it has become after the encounter with God.

WHAT DIFFERENCE DOES IT MAKE?

Some interesting theological issues appear in these three verses.

1. If the meaning of the psalm is that the writer had lived a life of pride, arrogance, prestige, and wealth, and then changed her lifestyle to focus more on the spiritual side of life, how did she move from here to there? What happened to turn her whole life around?

2. Among older persons the problem is usually not that of having too much pride or being arrogant. On the contrary, many experience a loss of self-esteem after retirement from work that was very important to them. However, there are some who are so proud of their life's accomplishments, the accomplishments of their children and grandchildren, and their own postretirement activities that the unwelcome experience of pride rears its ugly head. The question is: How much is too much, and how much is

too little? The psalmist was aware of her own arrogance, and found it not to be satisfying, so at the time of her writing the psalm it would seem that she has dealt with that problem and has been filled with humility in the presence of God. What would be a good balance in self-esteem and self-image?

3. What was hope to the writer of this psalm? What do you think "hope in the LORD" meant to her? When a person is active, healthy, and fully engaged in a satisfying life, what does "hope in the LORD" mean? Is the same meaning appropriate for a person who is experiencing some of the limitations brought on by the aging process? How about someone who is terminally ill; would the meaning of "hope in the LORD" differ?

This psalm also raises some personal issues.

1. In your own life have you ever experienced a "breakthrough," like the psalmist, from a very unsatisfying life to a peaceful, fulfilling life? What made the difference? What happened to cause the change?

2. On your own priority list where do you place material things? What is at the top of the list? What is midway down the list? What would you list at the bottom of the priority list of material things? How do you decide between what you need and what you want? Have you reached the point where material things and/or position have less meaning than they once did? If so, what brought about the change? If not, when do you anticipate that it will happen? When will you begin to "clear out the clutter"?

3. Remember when you were younger and fighting for your independence from parents and other authorities over your life. Then remember a time when you felt totally dependent upon forces or persons outside yourself. Have you ever felt that you did not have the inner strength to face a situation? Did you feel that you were totally dependent upon God at that point, or did you experience a surge of independence and resist being dependent? Does the idea that humans are not the independent beings we have always striven to be bother you? Does the idea of being totally dependent upon God bother you?

4. Ponder the image of the weaned child sitting calmly with its mother. If the image indicates that the psalmist wants only to be in the presence of God, not necessarily wanting anything from God, how do you feel about this image in your own life?

Do you always seek something from God, or is it enough just to be in God's presence?

PUTTING IT ALL TOGETHER
AND BRINGING IT HOME

The image of the weaned child sitting with its mother is the image of one who is still dependent upon the mother, but who is also beginning to experience some independence. One of the most poignant messages from this psalm for older adults has to do with how we view dependence and independence. As we stated previously, contrary to popular belief, dependence is not a four-letter word. It is a human word. Dependence is not some physical or emotional inadequacy indicating that dependent persons are less than what they ought to be. Dependency is a reality of life for all of us. We are born dependent and we remain that way all of our lives, not just when we are in our earlier years and in our later years.

The author of Psalm 71 says it this way: "Upon you I have leaned from my birth" (v. 6). So while defending and exercising our independence when it is appropriate, all of us of whatever age need to accept the gift God has given us, the gift of being able to depend on one another when we need it. Dependence is not a sign of weakness or failure; it is not a decree of worthlessness or uselessness. Dependence is part of God's plan; it is God's gift. The ability to be as independent as our limited selves can manage, the ability to depend on others when we need them— both are good gifts of a gracious God.

Some questions to ponder:

1. Where does this psalm touch your life?
2. What is the message of the psalm for you?
3. Describe what your life would be like if you lived each day just to be in the presence of God, not wanting anything from God. How would life be different than it is now?

HELPS FOR GROUP STUDY

A. Print out copies of various translations and/or paraphrases of Psalm 131 and have each read by a different person.

B. Compare the different translations and paraphrases, and discuss the different emphases in each. What is the difference in the moods?

C. Choose the key words and phrases and discuss their meaning. How do the differing interpretations of scholars enrich your understanding of these verses?

D. Identify some of the themes of the psalm. What was the central message that the writer was trying to get across to the reader? Why do you think she wrote the psalm?

E. Discuss what historical data or context can be discerned from the psalm itself. Does this information throw any light on the meaning of the psalm?

F. Discuss the meaning of each verse in the present world. Do they have a message for us today?

G. Discuss the theological issues and the personal issues raised.

H. Lead the group in discussing how the psalm touches their own lives.

I. Close with prayer, using Eugene Peterson's paraphrase of Psalm 131.[14]

Notes

1. William L. Holladay, *The Psalms through Three Thousand Years* (Minneapolis: Fortress Press, 1993), 40.

2. Ibid., 341.

3. *The New Interpreter's Bible,* vol. 4 (Nashville: Abingdon Press, 1996), 1208.

4. Artur Weiser, *The Psalms* (Philadelphia: Westminster Press, 1962), 776.

5. Eugene H. Peterson, *The Message: Psalms* (Colorado Springs: Nav Press, 1994), 237–38.

6. *New Interpreter's Bible,* 4:1208.

7. P. D. Miller, *They Cried to the Lord: The Form and Theology of Biblical Prayer* (Minneapolis: Fortress Press, 1994), 240.

8. Walter Brueggemann, *The Message of the Psalms: A Theological Commentary,* Old Testament Studies (Minneapolis: Augsburg Publishing House, 1984), 48.

9. Robert Davidson, *The Vitality of Worship: A Commentary on the*

Book of Psalms (Grand Rapids: Wm. B. Eerdmans Publishing Co., 1998), 427.

10. W. O. E. Oesterley, *The Psalms* (London: SPCK, 1959), 528.

11. Ibid., 529.

12. Brueggemann, *Message of the Psalms,* 49.

13. James L. Mays, *Psalms,* Interpretation: A Bible Commentary for Teaching and Preaching (Louisville, Ky.: John Knox Press, 1994), 408.

14. Peterson, *The Message: Psalms,* 180.

Chapter 10

Psalm 121
WHERE DO I GO FOR HELP?

In the midst of facing the troubles, trials, and tragedies of life, men and women throughout the ages have turned to the Psalms for comfort, guidance, and daily strength.
—Victor M. Parachin

INTRODUCTION

Like Psalm 23, Psalm 121 is one of the psalms we use in some of our most sacred liturgies. It is particularly known within the context of a service that witnesses to the resurrection. It is an incredible psalm that needs to be read very carefully, and with careful timing. The questions dealt with in this psalm could be: How can I maintain my life for the rest of my life? How can I find meaning and purpose for my life for the rest of my life? As we enter the twenty-first century, these two questions are in the minds of older adults as they confront the probability that they will live for another fifteen to twenty years or more past their retirement.[1] Perhaps some insights into the answers to these two questions can be found in a study of Psalm 121.

We began these psalm studies with a look at the experiences of the Israelites in exile in Babylon following the destruction of the temple in Jerusalem. We considered how many times we too feel as though we are in exile, separated from all that gives meaning to life, and moving on to a different stage in our lives in the midst of anxieties and grief over losses. We moved on to consider the question, Who am I anyway? We posed the question of who we are in relationship to creation, to God, and to the other creatures who are also part of the created world, and how

we human beings fit into the scheme of things. In chapter 4, we
looked at life as a roller coaster ride, where we sail along com-
fortably and peacefully for a while, and then all of a sudden find
ourselves on the down slope, absolutely sure that we will not
survive when we hit the bottom of the track.

Our reflections on Psalms 42 and 43 in chapter 5 helped us to
explore the experience of being in a place where we do not want
to be, and yearning for connection and communication with
God. In chapter 6, Psalm 71 helped us to explore possibilities for
what to do with the rest of our lives. As we pondered the things
that involved looking back on our lives, we may have discovered
some glitches where we did not make wise choices, and, in fact,
engaged in some wrongdoing. Psalm 51 led us into thinking
about seeking God's forgiveness and getting a new start. After
the tumult of studying those psalms, we came to Psalm 23, the
psalm of calm assurance, peace, and serenity in the sure knowledge of the love of God. Peace and security are the themes that
continued in our study of Psalm 131. Now in this chapter, we
can review all that we have studied before in the way of laments,
but at the same time, become reassured that help is available as
we are so beautifully reminded in Psalm 121.

Persons who have grown up or have lived a significant portion
of their lives around mountains can feel a special closeness to this
psalm. This psalm contains words that have made "hill-loving
Scots view their hills as symbols of God's power and protection."[2]
Presbyterians and others who have experienced the beauty of the
mountains of western North Carolina, especially those who have
spent time at Montreat, on the edge of the Blue Ridge Parkway,
cannot help but feel the presence of God among those hills. But
even those whose lives have been spent in the plains and the flat-
lands of the Midwest can identify with this psalm, as it speaks of
the continuous, uninterrupted, loving care that is ours when we
are connected with the Creator. *The New Interpreter's Bible* surmises that *hills* could refer to "an unspecified destination, as in
the contemporary idiom, 'head for the hills.' "[3]

Whatever the meaning of "hills," whether literal or metaphorical, all of us who have ever climbed a high mountain and
viewed the world from the top have gotten a perspective on the
world and ourselves that is hard to find in other settings. Some

years ago, I climbed Mount Fuji in Japan, all 12,395 feet of it, from near sea level to the snow-filled crater at the top. I arrived at the top in time to see the sunrise, and I shall never forget the beauty of standing above a small layer of clouds and watching the sun come up over the edge of the clouds. It was as though the whole world was opening up before my eyes, as if I were standing on tiptoe at the time of creation and watching it happen, giving me the feeling that all things were new. After such an experience it was easy for me to understand how the hills could be seen as the place where one could feel close to God.

The hymn "I to the Hills Will Lift My Eyes" (*The Presbyterian Hymnal,* 234) comes directly from Psalm 121, and uses most of the images and metaphors found in the psalm. The first verse speaks of hills and help, and of eyes gazing at the one from whom all help comes:

> I to the hills will lift my eyes;
>> From whence shall come my aid?
> My help is from the Lord alone,
>> Who heaven and earth has made.

The Heidelberg Catechism makes a statement about trust in the providence of God that provides a nice confessional commentary on Psalm 121. To believe in "God the Father Almighty, Maker of heaven and earth" is, the catechism teaches, to "trust in him so completely that I have no doubt that he will provide me with all things necessary for body and soul. Moreover, whatever evil he sends upon me in this troubled life he will turn to my good, for he is able to do it, being almighty God, and is determined to do it, being a faithful Father."[4]

WHAT DOES THE PSALM SAY?

Psalm 121

> I lift up my eyes to the hills—
>> from where will my help come?
> My help comes from the LORD,
>> who made heaven and earth.
> He will not let your foot be moved;
>> he who keeps you will not slumber.

He who keeps Israel
  will neither slumber nor sleep.
The LORD is your keeper;
  the LORD is your shade at your right hand.
The sun shall not strike you by day,
  nor the moon by night.
The LORD will keep you from all evil;
  he will keep your life.
The LORD will keep
  your going out and your coming in
  from this time on and forevermore.

Psalm 121 is the second in the Songs of Ascent that begin with Psalm 120 and continue through Psalm 134. Songs of Ascent were sung probably by travelers en route to Jerusalem, although there is no agreement among scholars as to the specific setting for the use of the psalm. At any rate, this psalm describes a strong trust that can go with a person on life's journey, assuring the traveler that he or she is not alone.

Since there is disagreement among scholars over not only the setting for the use of the psalm but the meaning of the various verses, it will be helpful to do a verse by verse exploration of possible meanings.

Verse 1: "I lift up my eyes to the hills—from where will my help come?" The psalm opens with a question that is answered in verse 2. If one does not pause after "hills," it sounds as though help comes from Jerusalem. Is it the temple? Is it the hills? The answer is neither: "My help comes from the LORD, who made heaven and earth."

Davidson points out that this could be a dialogue "between pilgrims and priests at the entrance to the temple."[5] However, others say it is the question of a traveler, perhaps en route to Jerusalem for a temple festival, traveling through danger zones filled with robbers. The question in this case refers to real anxiety, and seeks real strength to face the real dangers.

Weiser introduces a third possibility—that the psalmist is "communing with himself, quickening his religious sense by asking himself questions and giving his own answers."[6] (You, of course, may make your own interpretation of this verse.)

However, it makes sense that the psalm refers to the pilgrims on their way to Jerusalem, on a road that is fraught with dangers of all kinds. Further, it seems feasible that the crowd of travelers would chant verse 1, and their leader would answer their question with verse 2. There are times in our own lives when all of life is in chaos, filled with change and transition, and this question looms large. Where will we find the help we need to get through this trauma? Where can we turn to find support and sustenance that can be counted on? These pilgrims looked to the hills for whatever help would be forthcoming from the Creator God. It is as if the hills are alive with God's presence.

Verse 2: "My help comes from the LORD, who made heaven and earth." The answer to the question is that such help is available from the Lord, and what makes this a sure thing is that it is the same Lord who made heaven and earth. This Creator God watches over all of creation, and nothing is outside of God's loving care. This, of course, does not mean that the help is going to protect the traveler from every danger that lurks, but that the traveler is not alone in facing whatever comes. "This knowledge removes every doubt and provides firm ground for the comfort with which the speaker sets the traveler on his way," Weiser explains. This "trust in God's help is based on the idea of God's creative power . . . because all things are God's handiwork, God has the power to help whatever happens."[7]

Verses 3–4: "He will not let your foot be moved; he who keeps you will not slumber." Since the psalm is probably referring to a traveler on foot, there was the real danger of the foot slipping, causing the traveler to fall into deep crevices. For older adults the image of the foot slipping and causing one to fall is not only a metaphor that refers to slipping on the road along life's journey; it is a real fear as bones grow brittle and our sense of balance becomes less reliable.

Sometimes we also perceive that God is absent, that God has forgotten us or "gone to sleep." This verse gives positive assurance that the foot will not slip, and God will not slumber or sleep. It is significant to think of the continuation of the view of the Creator God. Weiser points out that the creation of the universe was not a one-time act, but is continuous. God continues to act in the world as a living God. "Creation and history, the past and the present, are welded into a unity, and it imparts to the latter the significance of an actual event which affects the life of the individual."[8]

Verses 5–6: "The LORD is your keeper; the LORD is your shade at your right hand. The sun shall not strike you by day, nor the moon by night."

Here "shade" obviously refers to protection from the sun by day and the moon by night. It was thought that sunstroke would occur if the traveler were not shaded, and that diseases would strike if he or she were not shaded at night. So again the assurance is reinforced with other metaphors that illustrate that whatever was needed on the journey, God was aware and would be involved in the solution.

It may be important to note that the promises given here are not given in great detail, but rather appear in the form of images and general statements. And, according to Mays, "the repetition of the verb 'keep' in the sense of 'guard,' 'protect' is used to compose a litany of assurance that says no more and no less than that 'the Lord will protect your soul everywhere always from every danger.'"[9]

Verses 7–8: "The LORD will keep you from all evil; he will keep your life. The LORD will keep your going out and your coming in from this time on and forevermore."

These verses make it clear that previous verses may well refer to an actual journey of pilgrims to Jerusalem, but that they also provide metaphors for the journey of life, and that whatever happens on that journey will be under God's watchful care. Whatever happens to us, whether we are going out or coming in, whether we are talking about today, tomorrow, or the end of this life, the psalmist proclaims that the Lord will keep us from all evil and will keep our life. That is impressive insurance coverage! It is certainly reminiscent of Romans 8:38: "For I am convinced that neither death, nor life, nor angels, nor rulers, nor things present, nor things to come, nor powers, nor height, nor depth, nor anything else in all creation, will be able to separate us from the love of God in Christ Jesus our Lord."

WHAT DOES THE PSALM MEAN?

Notice how many times the words *keep* or *keeper* are used in the psalm. In this context, *keep* means to be in continuous charge. Synonyms of *keep* are *retain, maintain, preserve, care for,* or *tend.* What is the meaning of *keeper* to you? Is *keeper* an appropriate word for what we expect from God on our life's journey?

In addition to the metaphor of the foot slipping, as described previously, another metaphor in this psalm is shade (verses 5–6). If you have ever been in the tropical sun without shade you will know how important shade is for survival. A few years ago, I was in what was then Zaire in Africa to attend the dedication ceremonies of the Good Shepherd Hospital at Kananga. The ceremonies were outside in the sun and lasted for hours. Those of us sitting in the audience had no shade of any kind. After about two hours of sitting in the blazing sun, I passed out and had to be revived and cooled off. The metaphor of shade denotes protection from anything that saps our life away or keeps us from being all that we are capable of being. How about the metaphor, "your going out and your coming in"? What does that conjure up in your mind about the nature of God's care? What other metaphors do you find in the psalm?

There are some interesting theological issues raised by this psalm. For example, what does the word *help* mean in verses 1 and 2? Does it mean that we don't have to worry about things because God will take care of everything? Does it mean that God is our own personal caregiver, and therefore nothing bad can happen to us? Probably the answer to both questions would be No. So what does the word *help* mean?

In verses 3 and 4, is it true that God is so personally involved with the traveler that God will protect the traveler from stumbling or slipping? Is God so personally involved in our lives that God can be counted on to keep us from stumbling into danger or wrongdoing, and to hold us up when we are apt to slip into the mire?

In verse 7, how can we match the words "the LORD will keep you from all evil" with the reality of evil in the world? Evil harms believers and unbelievers, and seems many times to appear in random acts with no clear cause; it just seems to be evil for evil's sake. And in verse 8, what does *keep* mean?

The personal issue that emerges from this psalm has to do with responsibility. If we count on God to protect, care for, tend to, and keep us "from this time on and forevermore," what is our responsibility on life's journey?

WHAT DIFFERENCE DOES IT MAKE?

The difference that Psalm 121 can make in our lives is that it presents in a beautiful, almost poetic manner, the simple yet profound expression of trust in God for guidance on the journey, at every turn, from beginning to end. We can rest assured that God does not leave us unattended at any time; God neither slumbers nor sleeps. The words *protection, guidance, safety,* form the basic message of the psalm. The final promise is that what Oesterley calls "guardianship and defense" from God will be with us "from this time on and forevermore."

PUTTING IT ALL TOGETHER
AND BRINGING IT HOME

The difference that this kind of promise can make in our lives is in leading us to live a life of praise to God for God's faithfulness; it can also lead us to live a life feeling secure and safe from both enemies and the elements. So, if we truly believe Psalm 121, why are we human beings not able to live lives as we should? Why is stress one of the major problems in today's hurried and very complex society, and why are diseases resulting from that stress at the top of the list of disabling and fatal diseases in our nation? How do we account (or can we?) for the disparity between God's faithful guardianship and the emotionally, spiritually, and sometimes physically disabling forces that affect our lives in this world? Where is the disconnect between the experience of the psalmist and the times in our lives when there just seems to be no stopping the intrusions of disease, despair, and various dislocations in human relationships and the human spirit? Is there something we do not yet see between the psalmist's faith and the hard realities of our own lives?

HELPS FOR GROUP STUDY

A. Read the eight verses of Psalm 121 antiphonally by dividing the group into two, with each group reading one verse at a time until the psalm is finished.

B. Read the psalm again, one at a time, until everyone has read one verse. (You may have to read the psalm many times over, depending on the size of the group.)

C. Identify the key words and images in the psalm. Why are these important?

D. What is the message the psalmist is seeking to communicate in the psalm?

E. Discuss the theological and personal issues raised by the psalm.

F. What is meant by the metaphor of shade in verse 5?

G. What might the message of the psalm be to the modern world?

H. Discuss the meaning of the words *keep* and *keeper,* and "your going out and your coming in." How can these images have meaning for our life's journey?

I. When was the last time you felt the need for a "keeper"? How were you "kept"?

J. What is the message of this psalm for where you are currently on your life's journey?

Notes

1. See "Growing in the Abundant Life," Report of the Task Force on Older Adult Ministry, adopted by the 204th General Assembly (1992), Presbyterian Church (U.S.A.), 1.

2. Robert Davidson, *The Vitality of Worship: A Commentary on the Book of Psalms* (Grand Rapids: Wm. B. Eerdmans Publishing Co., 1998), 408.

3. *The New Interpreter's Bible,* vol. 4 (Nashville: Abingdon Press, 1996), 1180.

4. Heidelberg Catechism, The Constitution of the Presbyterian Church (U.S.A.), Part I, *Book of Confessions* (Louisville, Ky.: Office of the General Assembly, 1996), 4.026.

5. Davidson, *Vitality of Worship,* 408.
6. Artur Weiser, *The Psalms* (Philadelphia: Westminster Press, 1962), 745.
7. Ibid., 747.
8. Ibid.
9. Mays, *Psalms,* 390.

Chapter 11

Psalm 147
HOW GOOD TO SING GOD'S PRAISES!

*Thus if the Bible also contains a prayer book, we
learn from this that not only that Word which he
has to say to us belongs to the Word of God, but also
that word which he wants to hear from us, because it
is the word of his beloved Son. . . . We can [speak
with him] by praying in the name of Jesus Christ.
The Psalms are given to us to that end, that we may
learn to pray them in the name of Jesus Christ.*
— Dietrich Bonhoeffer

INTRODUCTION

If you will listen to conversations around you, you will hear
people speak at great length of the negative side of the aging
process—at least, what they perceive to be the negative side. You
hear things like, "I just can't remember her name; I must be getting old." The truth is that the person probably never could remember names, even at a younger age. The negative stereotyping
of older adults, known as "ageism," runs rampant in our society,
even in the church. Aging is not accepted in a society that idol-
izes youth and youthfulness. Therefore, every effort is made to
deny aging, cover up its signs, and deceive ourselves that we will
never be "one of them."

However, there is another side to the aging process that is overlooked in our race toward looking and acting younger. Although
there is a downside to aging, it is not the only side. There are
advantages to becoming older. We only need to be open to
experiencing and recognizing them. There are new freedoms—

time, space, activities, opportunities, and choices—and new perspectives on life, including the ability to see endings as new beginnings. Una Kroll says it well: "I have learned . . . to adopt an attitude toward life that can blend the truth with a determination to enjoy what can be enjoyed, sidestep the problems that can be sidestepped and accept limitations where they cannot be avoided."[1]

Noted Dutch priest Henri Nouwen writes that "aging does not need to be hidden or denied, but can be understood, affirmed, and experienced as a process of growth by which the mystery of life is slowly revealed to us."[2] Kathleen Fischer faces the reality of aging when she observes that in reality aging is both descent and ascent, loss and gain, and this is true of growth at every stage of the life cycle. She says, "A spirituality of aging must help us find a way to turn losses into gains, to learn how the stripping process which often accompanies aging can be a gradual entrance into freedom and new life, how, in fact, aging can be winter grace."[3]

One of the puzzles of the modern world is what to call older persons. We are called "senior citizens," "golden agers," "older adults," "prime timers," and many other names. Helen Hayes called us "maturians," and Maggie Kuhn called us "the elders." If we focus more on the plus side of aging, perhaps the word *older* would not be such a no-no!

One of the pluses for some older adults is putting together the knowledge gained with experience and coming out with wisdom. Carroll Saussy defines wisdom as being able to "discover their direction in the midst of ambivalence," to "know the difference between substance and trivia," and to "know what is important and how to compromise."[4]

Another advantage suggested by Saussy is freedom—freedom from having so many things, freedom from feeling that you have to know all the answers, and "little concern about dogmatic claims that divide denominations or faith groups, and are able to embrace others with greater sincerity."[5] Still another plus is the desire and time to continue to be a learner. Colleges and universities are adding classes in response to the desire of older adults to continue their learning late into life. Elder Hostels are another context in which this learning takes place, and the Elder Hostel program is increasingly popular around the world.

Finally, a very important development for older persons is attention to our own health needs, and taking control of our health progress. Previously, when we got sick we went to the doctor to be healed. This is still true to a certain extent, but we can be and need to exhibit more control in making decisions about our own health care. Every time I go to a doctor I have at least two pages of questions to ask, written down. I want to know what is the problem, what are the options for dealing with it, and when do we start! This gives me a feeling of being more in control and not merely at the mercy of the physician.

I have come to believe that health is not what we have until we get sick, but health is something we work toward and pay special attention to all of our lives. There is more to health than the absence of disease. Health has to do with the fulfillment and wholeness that we strive for throughout our lives. It has to do with our ability to enjoy and participate fully in life no matter at what stage of life we find ourselves.

There are many examples of older persons who were experiencing physical limitations and health problems, but who accomplished amazing feats, perhaps their greatest, in their later years. Vladimir Horowitz, at the age of 81, was featured in a cover story in *Time* magazine telling of his outstanding piano concerts in Moscow and Leningrad. At 89 Arthur Rubenstein gave one of the most unbelievable concerts in the history of Carnegie Hall. Because of failing vision he could no longer see the keyboard or read the music, but he performed the entire concert, relying solely on his memory and touch.

An excellent example of a person who lives on the positive side of the aging process is John I. Rhea. He is 88 years of age at this writing, and has been a full-time volunteer in the Office on Older Adult Ministry of the Presbyterian Church (U.S.A.) for four years. He retired many years ago after serving for twenty-five years as a chaplain in the military. Subsequently, he was on the staff of the Board of Education for the Presbyterian Church, U.S., and after that was director of social agencies for the elderly for nineteen years. When he had completed all of that, he offered his services to the church at the age of 84. During these four years, he has spearheaded the creation of the National Association for Retired Ministers, Their Spouses and Survivors. With his leadership, the movement has gone from a good idea to a nationwide association that has already held two successful national conventions and is planning a third to celebrate the end and beginning of a millennium.

John Rhea sets a high standard for all of us older adults. He summarizes the contributing factors to his longevity as "a wonderful nurturing father and mother, a loving and supportive wife and daughter, a clear call from God to serve, an ability to deal positively with life's experiences, living an expanding life, good self-esteem, regular medical checkups, absence of fear of aging, a proper diet, regular exercise, and love of people of all ages and cultures." Somewhere along the way, John Rhea must have read Psalm 147 and decided to live by its exuberance.

One of the notable elders of our time is former President Jimmy Carter. In his latest book, *The Virtues of Aging* (1998), Carter identifies and reflects on the many factors and people that have contributed to his positive outlook on getting older, not the least of which is his grounding in faith and his lifelong involvement in a community of faith.

Many of the studies in this book have to do with psalms of lament, seeking the assurance of the presence of a caring God who can support us through difficult times, and finding ways to express gratitude to God for God's faithfulness in those "down" times. It seems appropriate in this last chapter to focus exclusively on praise to God for all the ways that God has found to bless, not only us personally, but all good things in God's creation; and for life itself, for our being allowed to live to a "good old age." This is an accomplishment in itself!

Psalm 147 is about praising God for God's restoring Jerusalem, for gathering up the exiles of Israel, for healing brokenness, and so on. It is fitting to end with this psalm because it encourages remembering what God has done, and gives thanks and praise to God for life, for bringing healing in times of brokenness, for providing hope in difficult times, and for making the wind to blow and the waters flow (v. 18).

With these thoughts in mind, let's now turn to a study of this psalm, which is a prayer of praise to God for God's goodness.

WHAT DOES THE PSALM SAY?

Psalm 147

Praise the LORD!
How good it is to sing praises to our God;
    for he is gracious, and a song of praise is fitting.
The LORD builds up Jerusalem;
    he gathers the outcasts of Israel.
He heals the brokenhearted,
    and binds up their wounds.
He determines the number of the stars;
    he gives to all of them their names.
Great is our Lord, and abundant in power;
    his understanding is beyond measure.
The LORD lifts up the downtrodden;
    he casts the wicked to the ground.
Sing to the LORD with thanksgiving;
    make melody to our God on the lyre.
He covers the heavens with clouds,
    prepares rain for the earth,
    makes grass grow on the hills.
He gives to the animals their food,
    and to the young ravens when they cry.
His delight is not in the strength of the horse,
    nor his pleasure in the speed of a runner;
but the LORD takes pleasure in those who fear him,
    in those who hope in his steadfast love.
Praise the LORD, O Jerusalem!
    Praise your God, O Zion!
For he strengthens the bars of your gates;
    he blesses your children within you.
He grants peace within your borders;
    he fills you with the finest of wheat.
He sends out his command to the earth;
    his word runs swiftly.
He gives snow like wool;
    he scatters frost like ashes.
He hurls down hail like crumbs—
    who can stand before his cold?

He sends out his word, and melts them;
    he makes his wind blow, and the waters flow.
He declares his word to Jacob,
    his statutes and ordinances to Israel.
He has not dealt thus with any other nation;
    they do not know his ordinances.
Praise the LORD!

In trying to understand what the psalm really says, it might be helpful to read several other translations and discuss differences.

1. Verse 10 in the NRSV reads "speed of a runner," whereas the NIV renders the text as "legs of a man." What are the implications of these differences?
2. Verse 13 in the NRSV reads "he blesses your children within you," and in the NIV, "blesses your people within you." Is there any difference in the meaning of the two interpretations?
3. Verse 1 in the RSV uses the word "seemly," whereas the NRSV and the NIV use "fitting," and the NEB uses the words "How pleasant to praise him!" Is this only a difference in shades of meaning, or is there something deeper to think about?

The major theme throughout this psalm is the fervent outpouring of gratitude to God for God's mighty works. The psalm is divided into three parts. First, the congregation is summoned to praise God for God's goodness in rebuilding Jerusalem and restoring the people who were in exile. Second, the congregation is called on to sing and pray to the God who sends the rain to make the earth rich and sumptuous, and for providing for the animals. Finally, Jerusalem is called on to praise God who has brought restoration to the city and to the people who have returned after the exile.

WHAT DOES THE PSALM MEAN?

In their volume on Psalms in the Cambridge Bible Commentary series, J. W. Rogerson and J. W. McKay surmise that on the basis of verses 2 ("The Lord builds up Jerusalem") and 3 ("He strengthens the bars of your gates"), the psalm was composed during the time of Nehemiah (c. 445 B.C.E.) when the walls of Jerusalem were being rebuilt and the city repopulated (Nehemiah 4–7).[6] The main point is that it is through God's love and grace for God's people that Israel has been restored and can praise and serve God.

The placement of Psalm 147 is intriguing. The final five psalms in the book of Psalms are all so-called "hallelujah psalms." What a beautiful plan for closing out the book of Psalms, with five rousing hymns of praise to God for God's mighty works. What a beautiful plan, as well, for older adults to view the last one-third of their lives as an opportunity to sing hymns of praise to God for the mighty acts of God in their lives!

The *NRSV Harper Study Bible* divides the psalm into three parts, each one beginning with a directive to do something followed by a number of reasons why the directive should be accomplished. The first division is about "The God of might in history" (vv. 1–6), and lists those things the Lord has done concerning the building up of Jerusalem: gathering the outcasts of Israel, healing the brokenhearted, and lifting up the downtrodden. The second division is entitled "The God who sustains life" (vv. 7–11). It has to do with bringing rain to the earth to make the grass grow, giving animals their food, and taking pleasure in those persons that "fear" the Lord. The third section is "Israel exhorted to praise God" (vv. 12–20), pointing to the military benefits that the Lord has wrought, such as granting peace.[7]

This division of ideas is helpful in discerning the meaning of the psalm for older adults. We too can look at "the God of might" in our own history and list those things God has done in our lives in building up, gathering the pieces of our lives, healing us, and lifting us up. Certainly we older adults know "the God who sustains life," bringing into our lives those people and experiences that help us to grow and to become all that we are capable of becoming. In the third section, we older adults can find many reasons to praise God, pointing especially to the peace that can come from being in a close relationship with this "God of might" who loves us.

An exploration of some of the verses will be helpful in seeking out what the psalm means.

1. Verse 1 sets the tone for the entire psalm: "How good it is to sing praises to our God; for he is gracious, and a song of praise is fitting." Because God is gracious, it is appropriate to sing praises to God. When you look at the list of items in the following verses for which to give praise, no wonder the psalmist shouts "Praise the Lord!" The temple has been rebuilt, the scattered people in exile have been brought back, those who have been through horrendous experiences have experienced the Lord's healing touch, and the wicked have been "cast to the ground." O happy day!

2. In verse 2, "builds up Jerusalem" may mean that God is continually caring for Jerusalem and its recovery. It may not mean that the temple has been completely restored, but that the people are on their way toward rebuilding, regathering, being healed, and putting things in proper order.

3. Verses 7–11 again provide a laundry list of reasons why the psalmist is encouraging the crowds to sing to the Lord with thanksgiving. The Lord brings the rain that makes the grass grow, provides food for the animals and birds, and delights in those who accept God's steadfast love.

4. Verse 12 continues the words of praise: "Praise the LORD, O Jerusalem!" Why should they praise the Lord? It is because God has strengthened the protective bars that guard the gates. God has brought peace within the borders. God has provided food. And God has put the natural order back in place so there is snow, frost, hail, wind, and waters flowing.

5. Following verse 15 there is a listing of some of the commands that God sent out, including the natural cycles of nature (frost, snow, hail, wind, waters), but also God's word, statutes, and ordinances.

In summary, the message of the psalm seems to be a directive to give thanks and to worship God for God's mighty acts in nature and toward all those who "fear" him. The psalmist lists the many reasons for praising God, for God's attention to those who are downtrodden, brokenhearted, and wounded—for the whole of creation and the orderliness of what God has made.

WHAT DIFFERENCE DOES IT MAKE?

Some theological issues are raised that are worth identifying:

Following the exile, when the people were returning to Jerusalem, they needed healing, both physically and spiritually. The psalmist indicates that God brought the needed healing to the people. In verse 6, the psalmist makes a general statement that "The LORD lifts up the downtrodden; he casts the wicked to the ground." When this does not happen in life, what are the theological implications? Was the psalmist being overzealous in the general statement? How can we in our time view all the evil in the world, and the fact that the poor and the downtrodden are still with us, in light of this psalm?

Verse 20 indicates that God has not dealt this way with any other nation, that they do not know God's ordinances. However, Psalm 96 speaks of the whole world when it says: "Declare his glory among the nations, his marvelous works among all the peoples . . . Say among the nations, 'The LORD is king!' " (vv. 3, 10). Obviously, the author of this psalm saw the situation in a different light.

There are also some significant personal issues that need exploration:

1. For persons who have had only troubles and struggles in their lives, who do not feel that they have experienced the graciousness and the greatness of God, what meaning can this psalm have?

2. If, as the psalmist writes, God sends the snow, hail, wind, and waters, how can those who have been devastated by heavy snows, hail, or strong winds and floods praise God?

PUTTING IT ALL TOGETHER
AND BRINGING IT HOME

1. Name some of the blessings that you have experienced and for which you can fervently praise God for God's goodness. What are some of the positive features of the later years that

you have experienced? What are some of the adjectives you
would use to describe your own old age?

2. What special gifts has God given to you during the last five
years for which you are deeply grateful to God?

3. What brings you the greatest pleasure in your life as an
older person, and for which you sing praises to God?

4. As you look to the future, what gifts of God do you expect
to claim and experience for yourself?

5. What is the message of this psalm for you today?

6. What are the new freedoms that you experience at your
present age?

7. What do you know now that you did not know twenty
years ago concerning how to live life?

8. In what ways can you pass on to the next generation the
wisdom of your years?

9. Would you really want to be young again?

HELPS FOR GROUP STUDY

A. Choose three readers among the class members and ask
the first one to read verses 1–6, the second to read verses
7–11, and the third to read verses 12–20.

B. Read the chapter once again, one verse at a time, from
the different translations, and discuss the differences.

C. Identify what the group sees to be key words, phrases,
and images, and discuss their meaning.

D. Identify and discuss the themes.

E. Have someone in the group summarize what the
psalmist might have been saying to the people of his
day.

F. Have someone in the group summarize what might be
the message of the psalm for the people of today.

G. Make a list of the experiences of celebration in the lives
of the members of the class, and project into the future
to name those blessings and celebrations that are antic-
ipated.

H. Think of a person who is older than you are, whom you respect and honor, and on whom you would like to model your own life in the later years. What are the attributes that cause you to respect and honor that person? What adjectives would you choose to describe the person? What are the barriers that would keep you from using that person as a model? What is the first thing you will do to begin that modeling?

I. End by singing the Doxology.

Notes

1. Una Kroll, *Growing Older* (Glasgow: William Collins Sons & Co., 1988), 52.

2. Henri Nouwen and Walter J. Gaffney, *Aging* (Garden City, N.Y.: Image Books, 1974), 14.

3. Kathleen Fischer, *Winter Grace: Spirituality for the Later Years* (New York: Paulist Press, 1985), 4.

4. Carroll Saussy, *The Art of Growing Old: A Guide to Faithful Aging* (Minneapolis: Augsburg, 1998), 75.

5. Ibid., 77.

6. J. W. Rogerson and J. W. McKay, *Psalms*, The Cambridge Bible Commentary (Cambridge and New York: Cambridge University Press, 1977), 148.

7. *NRSV Harper Study Bible,* expanded and updated (Grand Rapids: Zondervan Publishing House, 1991), 900.

POSTSCRIPT

As a book for pilgrims, the Psalms transcend limitations of time and space. Reading the Psalms implies simultaneously two congregations. . . .The first are those pilgrims of ancient Israel who expressed in the Psalms their journey to the God of Israel. The second are pilgrims who throughout all time and in all places journey to God through praying.

—Mark S. Smith

As we come to the end of these psalm studies there are some additional thoughts I would like to share. This study has stimulated my thinking on many fronts, and I hope it has done the same for you. The first thought I want to share has to do with what I experienced as I went through the study of these ten psalms. One question that has continued to cause me concern and consternation is the question of theodicy. In other words, how is it that God is all-powerful and all-loving, and yet the world is filled with pain and anguish? If God is all-powerful, why does God not intervene, overrule, and cause the pain to cease?

Psalm 103:3–5 refers to the God "who forgives all your iniquity, who heals all your diseases, who redeems your life from the Pit, who crowns you with steadfast love and mercy, who satisfies you with good as long as you live so that your youth is renewed like the eagle's." Where is the reality in those words? The world in which I live does not include the experience that God heals all diseases, redeems my life from the Pit, or satisfies me with good as long as I live. If there is truth in these words, where have we gone wrong? If there is truth here why are there so many unhealed diseases, why do so many of us spend so much time in the Pit, and why do so many bad things happen to good people? How can we merge what we read in the Psalms with what we experience in life?

I have struggled with this question for years, and working through these psalms has helped me to come out with a workable theory. I have concluded that God created all that is, the world and all that is in the world as we know it, and the whole universe, including human beings. Being all-powerful and loving, God made human beings with freedom of choice. God loved human beings enough to risk it all by giving humans responsibility, not only for themselves and their own lives, but responsibility for (or dominion over) everything that was made. In the use and abuse of that freedom humans have themselves created situations that bring upon themselves most of the difficulties, the struggles, the illnesses, and the traumas that we deal with every day.

However, we tend to blame God for bringing on the struggles, as did the psalmist: "My God, my God, why have you forsaken me? Why are you so far from helping me, from the words of my groaning?" (22:1). We abuse the environment and wonder why we get sick. We smoke cigarettes and wonder why we get lung cancer. We live in stressful environments daily and wonder why our bodies rebel. We mix drinking and driving, and when an accident occurs we hear people say, "It was God's will," or "His time had come," when the truth of the matter is that when we make unwise judgments there are sure to be tragic consequences. The problem is that we have not understood Psalm 8 correctly. *Dominion* does not mean "I can do anything with the created world that I want to do for my own satisfaction." It means that we are stewards of the created world, to care for it, tend it, and maintain it with love. This includes caring for, tending, and maintaining with love that part of creation that is made up of other human beings, the human environment.

The same is true of the care of our bodies. "Do you not know that your body is a temple of the Holy Spirit within you, which you have from God, and that you are not your own? For you were bought with a price; therefore glorify God in your body"

(1 Corinthians 6:19–20). If we truly cared for our physical bodies all of our lives, we would avoid many, if not most, of the illnesses that come to us in our younger years, but especially in our later years.

My father died of a heart attack at the age of 79. An earlier heart attack some ten years before had been quite serious and had caused extensive damage to his heart. After the first heart attack he really took care of himself, followed all the rules set down by the doctor, ate right, exercised, handled stress in healthy ways, enjoyed his life to the fullest, and lived another ten years. He said after his first attack that if he had known before what he knew after, he would never have had the first heart attack. The problem is that these days we do know what is good for us and what is bad for us, but we say to ourselves, "It'll never happen to me." Some scientists are suggesting these days that if we really took care of ourselves the term *life expectancy* would go out of existence; because there would not be an ultimate life expectancy. Already the projection is that the natural life span is 120 years, and within the near future people who live to be 120 will not be an exception.

In the meantime, we live in the real world where human beings make bad choices, and we have to live with the consequences. The good news is that God suffers with us, even though we bring pain and suffering on ourselves. God is right there with us, bringing comfort, strength, and wisdom for the difficult times, just as God was with the exiles in Babylon who asked the question, "How could we sing the LORD's song in a foreign land?" (Psalm 137:4). The psalmist keeps this reality before us, that "God is our refuge and strength, a very present help in trouble. Therefore we will not fear, though the earth should change" (46:1–2).

Not only is God with us in the struggles, but God forgives us, as we discovered in Psalm 51, when we repent of our wrong decisions and come to God asking for forgiveness. God will indeed "Create in me a clean heart . . . and put a new and right spirit within me" (51:10).

Walter Brueggemann's approach to this question has been helpful to me. He says, "our faith moves from being securely oriented to being painfully disoriented, and finally to being surprisingly reoriented."[1] Although Brueggemann is thinking more of how everyone is in transit from the flow of orientation, disorientation, and reorientation, this experience seems to be especially true for older persons. We go through times of being disoriented by our losses and dislocations, but invariably these become opportunities for new beginnings. Aging is not a destination. It is a journey, and we never arrive in this life.

Another question that I have struggled with throughout this study is this: How does the psalmist move so rapidly from the depths of despair to the heights of ecstasy? I have come out truly believing that when we get to the end of our rope, feeling that all is lost and that even God has abandoned us, we almost always run back to God and ask for help. It is usually the last thing we think of doing. However, as we consider the nature of God and how God has delivered us from the Pit, we begin to have the faith that God is with us, loves us, and will not forsake us. Therein lies the secret to life on the roller coaster. As Psalm 42:11 exclaims with determination: "Hope in God, for I shall again praise him, my help and my God." Paul Tillich, in *The New Being,* gives us a glimpse into how this happens: "We want only to communicate to you an experience we have had that here and there in the world and now and then in ourselves is a New Creation, usually hidden, but sometimes manifest, and certainly manifest in Jesus who is called the Christ."[2]

In our studies through the ten psalms we have been on a pilgrimage. In ancient days people went to Jerusalem on their pilgrimage. The focus was worship in the temple. But the point of the pilgrimage is not the destination, it is the journey itself. It is being "on the way," and in the traveling together we discover what it means to be a pilgrim and why we are on the journey.

On vacations we go to places. Pilgrims don't go to places. As someone once said, "Pilgrims let places pass through them." This means that the important point is what we discover on the way, and how we are changed by what we discover. What is important is what we found together as we journeyed through the Psalms, and what we find together as we journey through this pilgrimage called aging.

Although Psalm 134 was not selected for study, I will mention it because it represents the closing service or night vigil. There will be a closing service for us, and there will be many night vigils. The call is to bless God by singing songs of praise. Lifting up our holy hands to the holy place, the call is to respond to what we have discovered about God, to offer praise about what we have discovered about ourselves and about God on the journey. The effect of offering this praise is to receive the power of God's blessing. The more we discover about God the more we want to go on discovering about God, and the more we want to praise God. The more we talk about our faith and the truths that we have discovered, the more we struggle to put into words the insights we have gathered, the more we will realize how profound these truths are. As we tell the story, it becomes clearer to us and its meaning is revealed. In Psalm 134 the psalmist offers this liturgy:

> Come, bless the LORD, all you servants of the LORD,
>> who stand by night in the house of the LORD!
> Lift up your hands to the holy place,
>> and bless the LORD.
> May the LORD, maker of heaven and earth,
>> bless you from Zion.

My hope is that you have used this book in a group study. If so, the point of your study was not that you studied the psalms on this journey, but that you did it together. In the original Bible study in the retirement community cited at the beginning of this book, the important thing was that in studying the psalms together we learned new things about each other, about ourselves, about God, and about God's pilgrimage with us in community. If you have done the study individually, I hope that you will find a way to share your pilgrimage with friends and continue to learn together about the value of the journey in community.

As we enter the twenty-first century we are discovering some things about aging that we didn't know before. The science and medicine that we thought were the ultimate answers, we now discover are only part of the truth. The temptation is still to seek the definitive answer, the final and unchanging answer to all our questions. However, the Hebrew scriptures are about the journey, about the companionship of God with us on the journey.

In between the beginning and the ending of the journey God invites us to *Solvitu Ram-bulando,* a Latin phrase meaning, "the way is solved in the traveling."

Notes

1. Walter Brueggemann, *Praying the Psalms* (Winona, Minn.: St. Mary's Press, 1982), 16.
2. Paul Tillich, *The New Being* (New York: Charles Scribner's Sons, 1955), 18.

BIBLIOGRAPHY

Alter, Robert. *Translation and Commentary on Genesis*. New York: W. W. Norton & Co., 1996.

Anderson, A. A. *Psalms*. The New Century Bible Commentary, vol. 1. Grand Rapids: Wm. B. Eerdmans Publishing Co. and London: Marshall, Morgan & Scott Publishing, 1972.

"A Brief Statement of Faith." Presbyterian Church (U.S.A.). 1994.

Briggs, Charles A., and Emilie Grace Briggs. *The Book of Psalms*. International Critical Commentary. Edinburgh: T. & T. Clark, 1976.

Brueggemann, Walter. *The Message of the Psalms: A Theological Commentary*. Old Testament Studies. Minneapolis: Augsburg Publishing House, 1984.

————. *Praying the Psalms*. Winona, Minn.: St. Mary's Press, 1982.

Davidson, Robert. *The Vitality of Worship: A Commentary on the Book of Psalms*. Grand Rapids: Wm. B. Eerdmans Publishing Co., 1998.

Day, John. *Psalms*. Sheffield: JSOT Press, 1992.

Fischer, Kathleen. *Winter Grace: Spirituality for the Later Years*. New York: Paulist Press, 1985.

"Growing in the Abundant Life," Report of the Task Force on Older Adult Ministry, adopted by the 204th General Assembly (1992), Presbyterian Church (U.S.A.).

Holladay, William L. *The Psalms through Three Thousand Years*. Minneapolis: Fortress Press, 1993.

The Interpreter's Dictionary of the Bible. Nashville: Abingdon Press, 1962.

Kalajainen, Larry R. *Psalms for the Journey*. Nashville: Upper Room Books, 1996.

Knight, George A. F. *Psalms*. Vol. 1 of The Daily Study Bible. Philadelphia: Westminster Press, 1982.

Kroll, Una. *Growing Older*. Glasgow: William Collins Sons & Co., 1988.

Lockyer, Herbert. *God's Book of Poetry*. Nashville: Thomas Nelson Publishers, 1983.

Mays, James L. *Psalms*. Interpretation: A Bible Commentary for Teaching and Preaching. Louisville, Ky.: John Knox Press, 1994.

Miller, P. D. *They Cried to the Lord: The Form and Theology of Biblical Prayer*. Minneapolis: Fortress Press, 1994.

The New Interpreter's Bible, vol. 4. Nashville: Abingdon Press, 1996.

NRSV Harper Study Bible. Expanded and updated. Grand Rapids: Zondervan Publishing House, 1991.

Nouwen, Henri, and Walter J. Gaffney. *Aging*. Garden City, N.Y.: Image Books, 1974.

Oesterley, W. O. E. *The Psalms*. London: SPCK, 1959.

The Oxford Dictionary of Current English. Oxford and New York: Oxford University Press, 1996.

Peterson, Eugene H. *The Message: Psalms*. Colorado Springs: Nav Press, 1994.

Rhodes, Arnold B. *Psalms*. The Layman's Bible Commentary. Atlanta: John Knox Press, 1960.

Rogerson, J. W., and J. W. McKay, commentary by. *Psalms*. The Cambridge Bible Commentary. Cambridge and New York: Cambridge University Press, 1977.

Saussy, Carroll. *The Art of Growing Old: A Guide to Faithful Aging*. Minneapolis: Augsburg, 1998.

Weber, Hans-Ruedi. *Experiments with Bible Study*. Philadelphia: Westminster Press, 1981.

Weiser, Artur. *The Psalms*. Philadelphia: Westminster Press, 1962.